IRON FIST

THE BOOK OF
CHANGES

ASSISTANT EDITORS:
Mark Powers (MCP #111-133 & NAMOR ANNUAL),
Mike Kraiger (MCP #134-141) &
Mark Bernardo (SPIDER-MAN)
EDITORS:
Terry Kavanagh (MCP #111-133 & NAMOR ANNUAL),
Richard Ashford (MCP #134-141) &
Danny Fingeroth (SPIDER-MAN)

FRONT COVER ARTISTS:
Sam Kieth & Veronica Gandini

BACK COVER ARTIST:
Steve Lightle

COLLECTION EDITOR: **MARK D. BEAZLEY** | ASSISTANT EDITOR: **CAITLIN O'CONNELL**
ASSOCIATE MANAGING EDITOR: **KATERI WOODY** | ASSOCIATE MANAGER, DIGITAL ASSETS: **JOE HOCHSTEIN**
SENIOR EDITOR, SPECIAL PROJECTS: **JENNIFER GRÜNWALD** | VP PRODUCTION & SPECIAL PROJECTS: **JEFF YOUNGQUIST**
RESEARCH & LAYOUT: **JEPH YORK** | PRODUCTION: **COLORTEK & JOE FRONTIRRE** | BOOK DESIGNER: **RODOLFO MURAGUCHI**
SVP PRINT, SALES & MARKETING: **DAVID GABRIEL**

EDITOR IN CHIEF: **AXEL ALONSO** | CHIEF CREATIVE OFFICER: **JOE QUESADA**
PRESIDENT: **DAN BUCKLEY** | EXECUTIVE PRODUCER: **ALAN FINE**

IRON FIST

THE BOOK OF CHANGES

YOU HAVE THE RIGHT TO REMAIN SILENT. ANYTHING YOU SAY CAN AND WILL BE USED A-GAINST YOU IN A COURT OF LAW...

OWW!

THAT, TOO.

WILL YOU WANT TO TESTIFY, MR. AH... *FIST*?

I DON'T KNOW WHY NO ONE ELSE NOTICES ANYTHING...

...BUT THAT *NOISE* IS FILLING MY HEAD, RINGING LOUDER THAN THE TEMPLE BELLS OF LOST K'UN L'UN!

THE CLOSER I GET TO THIS OLD CHURCH, THE STRONGER IT BECOMES!

IT'S GROWING CLEARER. IS IT A HUM... OR SOME STRANGE CHANT?

ST. MARK'S

IT'S NOT MERE CURIOSITY THAT COMPELS ME FORWARD...

I FEEL... *DRAWN* TO THIS PLACE.

ST. MAR

I DON'T THINK I COULD TURN AROUND NOW IF I WANTED TO!

THERE IS *MAGIC* AT WORK WITHIN! DO I DARE MEET IT?

DO I HAVE A *CHOICE*?

5

8

WHERE DID *HE* COME FROM? WHO LET HIM IN?

I ASSURE YOU, ABBOT, I HAD NO *IDEA*--

NEVER MIND, IDIOT! HE MUST NOT BE ALLOWED TO LEAVE! SUR-ROUND HIM! CAPTURE HIM!

BETTER MEN THAN YOU HAVE TRIED TO BRING ME DOWN.

BUT I'M STILL *VERY MUCH* ALIVE. MORE ALIVE THAN THESE SORRY SPEC-IMENS, AT ANY RATE

THE ONLY MUMMIES IN MANHATTAN BELONG IN A *MUSEUM!*

WHOKK

GOT TO PULL MY PUNCHES AGAINST THESE LIVING DEAD MEN! THEY'RE ONLY PUPPETS OF THE ABBOT, AFTER ALL!

CHUKK

THOK

IF I GIVE YOU CREDIT -- YOU TAKE A THRASHING BUT KEEP COMING.

I DON'T KNOW WHETHER THAT'S *YOUR* STAMINA... OR THE POWER OF THANADEMOS!

CHIK

CHUFF

SPEAKING OF YOUR BOSS, WHERE DOES HE THINK HE'S GOING?

I WOULDN'T WANT HIM TO *MISS* ANY OF THIS!

ENOUGH! I CAN SEE THIS IS A LOSING BATTLE! MY DAY WILL COME SOON ENOUGH!

NOW THAT I KNOW THE MAGICKS CONTAINED HEREIN WILL WORK --

-- I CAN RAISE *MULTITUDES* OF THE NEAR-DEAD... FROM SICKBEDS AND HOSPITALS ALL OVER THE CITY! THEY WILL YET BE MINE TO COMMAND... TO *ENSLAVE!*

I WILL HAVE AN *ARMY* AT MY DISPOSAL...

TOME OF

...WHEN I FIGHT AGAIN -- ANOTHER TIME!

NO TIME TO CHASE HIM --

-- AND HIS FOLLOWERS WOULDN'T LET ME ANYWAY!

KRAK

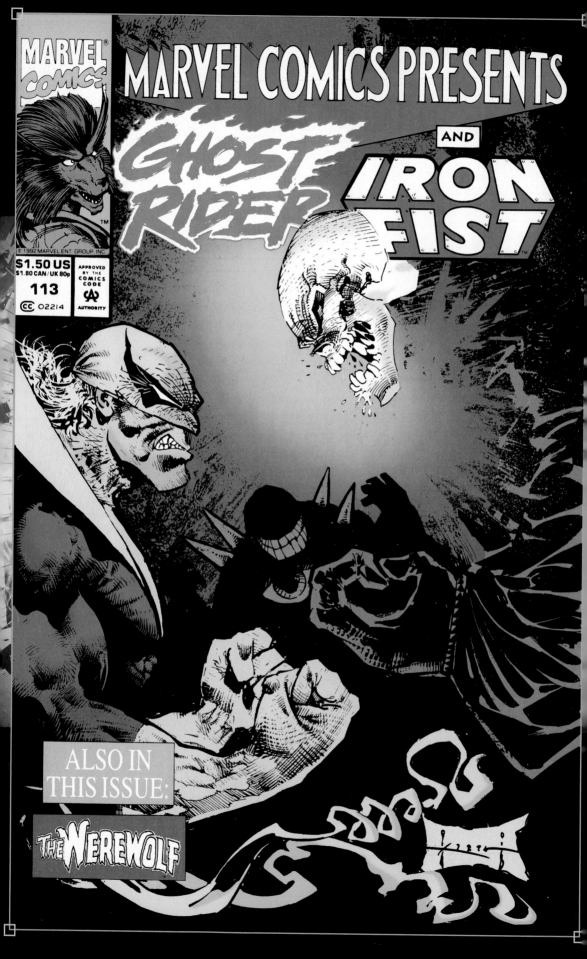

LEGION OF VENGEANCE
Part ONE

FEATURING

GHOST RIDER

AND

IRON FIST

Sometimes, Danny Ketch wishes he were not so observant.

Those secrets that hide on the periphery of our existence are all too clear to him.

Shadows that skitter and skulk into the enveloping darkness to escape our notice befriend him.

FEEL LIKE THE TRAIN'S A BIG BROTHER GUIDIN' ME HOME. LIKE IT *WANTS* ME TO GO HOME.

I STAY OUT LATER AND LATER JUST RIDING AROUND... TRYING TO MAKE SOME SENSE OF MY LIFE... MY *FUTURE*.

...BUT THE *PIECES* NEVER SEEM TO...

...TO FALL TOGETHER.

YO, WHAT WAS *THAT?*

SOME WISE GUY UP THERE, DROPPIN' STUFF DOWN FROM THE EL? DROPPING MONEY DOWN?

WELL, IF YOU WANTED MY *ATTENTION,* YOU GOT IT!

He could choose to ignore the pieces, but no matter how he tried, they would rise to meet so many others, for...

THE NIGHT HAS A THOUSAND EYES!

THIS STORY OCCURS BEFORE GHOST RIDER #25. --T.K.

13

14

17

18

AN ORDERLY RITE OF FAITH-- TURNED TO COMPLETE *CHAOS* BY THAT... *FANATIC.*

NO ONE CAN RAISE A *HAND* AGAINST HER...

...BUT I CAN RAISE A *FIST*-- --AN *IRON FIST!*

WHAT TREACHERY DOES THAT *MASK* HIDE?

MY FLAME WILL SHINE THE LIGHT OF *TRUTH* ON THE MAN BEHIND IT!

WRUNNNCH

VOOOM

IT SEEMS TO PUNISH THE *INNOCENT* AS WELL!

NO SECRET CAN WITHSTAND ITS *WHITE-HOT SCRUTINY!*

THE WHOLE CHURCH IS COMING DOWN AROUND US! WE GOTTA GET *OUT!*

EEEEEE

MAMA!

THE GUILTY WILL SUFFER THE HEAT OF *PURIFICATION!*

WAIT! THERE ARE STILL SOME PEOPLE TRAPPED BEHIND US!

19

22

CYPRESS HILLS... THE GRAVEYARD... GUYS IN TRICK OR TREAT COSTUMES... JUST LIKE *YOURS*...

COUGH THE OTHERS! THEIR FACES... BURSTING OPEN... *RIVERS OF PUS*... AND VIRUSES...

YOU CAN'T HELP ME...

BUT THE OTHERS! THE OTH--

MY TIME HAS BEEN *WASTED* HERE.

EVIL RUNS *RAMPANT*-- THREATENING THE INNOCENT! I'LL SPAR NO MORE WITH THE LIKES OF YOU!

"SPAR"? IS THAT ALL YOU THINK I AM CAPABLE OF?

THERE IS NO-WHERE YOU CAN GO, MISTER... THAT *IRON FIST* CANNOT FOLLOW!

WHAT DO YOU KNOW ABOUT THIS PLACE? THIS... WHAT DID HE CALL THE GRAVE-YARD?

CYPRESS HILLS.

KNOW *THIS*, HUMAN CALLED "IRON FIST"...

...IF THE *GHOST RIDER'S* TORTURED FRAME HELD A *SOUL*--

"--IT WOULD BE TO *THAT* CEMETERY TRULY BOUND *FOREVER!*"

AW, C'MON, DEB... ...WHO'S GONNA *SEE?*

I WILL *SEE*.

THE MIND'S EYE SEES *EVERYTHING*.

YOU PRACTICE *DECEIT* AND *TREACHERY*... OR YOU WOULD NOT COME TO SUCH A PLACE AS THIS TO *HIDE!*

PUNISHMENT IS CALLED FOR... ADMINISTERED BY--

--BACILLUS, CONTROLLER OF CONTAGION! MASTER OF *MICROBES!*

...HIS VERY *TOUCH* BRINGS... *SICKNESS*... *DISEASE*... *INFECTION!*

NO! *NO!* KEEP HIM AWAY FROM ME! I... WE... DON'T *DESERVE* THIS!

CYPRESS HILLS IS A PLACE WHERE THE DEAD ARE BROUGHT BY THE *LIVING*...

...NOT WHERE THE LIVING CREATE MORE *DEAD!*

CAN FEEL...MY OWN *BLOOD*... *CHURNING* INSIDE ME!..

...TEMPERATURE RISING... MAKING MY HEAD SWIM!

...HEAD FEELS... LIKE ITS GOING TO EXPLODE!

IF ONLY I HADN'T USED MY LIVING WEAPON POWER ON THE GHOST RIDER'S CYCLE! I MIGHT BE ABLE TO CURE MYSELF WITH IT!

BUT...IT TAKES... TIME...

...TO RESTORE IT TO... FULL CAPACITY!

THEY'RE GETTING AWAY... THIS IS *MY* FAULT!

THERE IS NO NEED TO BLAME YOURSELF!

NONE CAN HIDE FROM ME FOR LONG!

BUT FOR YOU, IRON FIST...

...LET US SEE TO IT THAT THIS GRAVEYARD DOES NOT BECOME YOUR FINAL RESTING PLACE YET.

AT THE SAME TIME...

--NOW AND AT THE HOUR OF OUR DEATH... AMEN.

LORD, HEAR OUR PLEA...YOUR FAITHFUL HAVE TAKEN THEIR VIGIL TO THE STREETS...

PLEASE HEAR OUR PRAYERS... INSTILL IN YOUR FOLLOWERS THE PEACE OF FORGIVENESS TO REPLACE THE ANGER AND OUTRAGE WE FEEL AT OUR LOSS!

...TO HONOR THE DEAD OF THE PARISH OF SAINT ALFONSO'S, AND TO PROTECT US AGAINST THE UNHOLY SCOURGE THAT ATTACKED YOUR SACRED HOME.

WHAT ABOUT OUR OUTRAGE?

PEOPLE IN THIS COMMUNITY HAVE DIED... AND WHAT IS THIS CITY DOING ABOUT IT?

THEY'LL PAY FOR IGNORING US!

WE'LL MAKE THEM PAY!

PAY?? YOUR SENSE OF OUTRAGE HAS A BOTTOM LINE... A PROFIT MOTIVE?

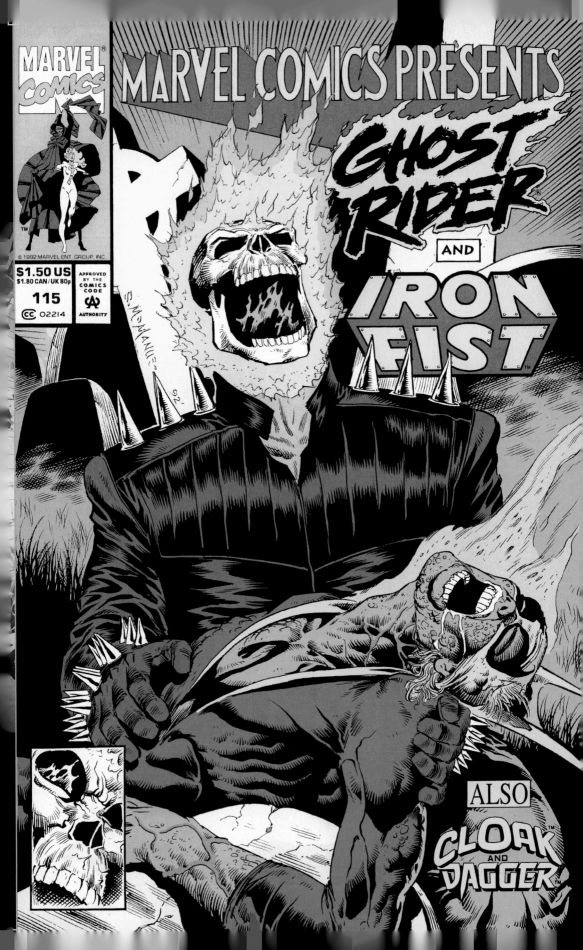

GET 'EM BEFORE THEY CAN *POISON* ANYBODY ELSE!

MISTAKEN IDENTITY.

THIS GETS *OLD FAST!*

THEY ARE *NOT MISTAKEN.* THEY WANT A TARGET FOR THEIR RAGE...AND THEY HAVE FOUND IT IN *US!*

YOU LOOK LIKE YOU GOT A DOSE OF THE SAME MEDICINE!

HOWZIT FEEL BEIN' ON THE RECEIVING END?

I *WAS* INFECTED, TOO, BY THE MANIAC CALLED *BACILLUS.* IF I DON'T BREAK FREE OF THIS MOB AND *FIND* HIM...I'LL *DIE!*

THEY BUILD THESE ICONS TO PIETY AND HOLINESS...

...AND USE THEM TO MASK THEIR *TRUE* FEELINGS OF GREED AND POWER LUST!

VESPER WILL ENSURE THAT THEY CAN NEVER HIDE BEHIND THEM AGAIN!

FOR WHEN HYPOCRISY RULES...*CHAOS MUST FOLLOW!*

KRAKOOM

NOT TODAY!

HA! TODAY... AND *FOREVER AFTER*, IF *OUR* WILL BE DONE!

OUR WORK IS *COMPLETE* FOR THIS NIGHT! LET US *RETURN* TO OUR *SANCTUM*... AND LET THE MASSES DEAL WITH THOSE *SANCTIMONIOUS POSERS* WHO DARED STOP US!

WHILE WE FADE INTO THE NIGHT!

RIGHT. THE *CROWD'LL* KEEP 'EM *BUSY*--

STAND AWAY FROM IRON FIST--

--OR CONFRONT A *POWER*--

--BEYOND YOUR *GRAVEST* IMAGININGS!

VZZZZZ

THOSE CHAIN LINKS! THEY'RE..

VZOK

ZOK

--THROWING *STARS*!

WHERE ARE WE GOING?

VESPER MENTIONED SOMETHING ABOUT A "SANCTUM"... SOME UNHOLY RETREAT THEY KEEP, NO DOUBT.

THE FOOTSTEPS OF THE ONE CALLED STRONTIUM-90 ARE EASILY TRACEABLE.

HUNH? A RADIOACTIVE TRAIL'S NOT VISIBLE TO THE NAKED EYE. HOW CAN--?

NOTHING ESCAPES ME.

YOU PROMISED ME ONCE THAT THIS CEMETERY WOULD NOT BECOME MY FINAL RESTING PLACE.

BUT STILL IT MIGHT BE.

BACILLUS'S INFECTION IS STILL RAGING THROUGH MY SYSTEM. ONLY MY K'UN L'UN TRAINING IS KEEPING ME FROM SUCCUMBING TO IT!

MY OWN POWER OF THE LIVING WEAPON WOULD HEAL ME... BUT SINCE I'VE ALREADY TRIED USING IT UNWISELY ON YOU AND VESPER... THE POWER'S DENIED ME FOR A TIME! BY THEN, I COULD BE DEAD!

FEAR NOT. THE TRAIL HAS REACHED ITS END.

DEAD END, YOU MEAN. THAT MAUSOLEUM DOOR IS SOLID STONE. IMPOSSIBLE TO OPEN!

IMPOSSIBLE? I AM A CREATURE OF THE IMPOSSIBLE!

WHA-BLAMM

GRIM UNDERTAKINGS REQUIRE GRIM SURROUNDINGS! THE TREACHERY THAT WAITS WITHIN THESE WALLS...

...CANNOT BE CONTAINED BY MERE STONE!

IT'S... IT'S...

CONTINUES NEXT ISSUE...

38

LEGION OF VENGEANCE
FEATURING
GHOST RIDER and IRON FIST

PART 4: OUR NAME IS

LEGION...

SO... BEFORE HE CAN GRAB ME--

--I'LL TAKE THE INITIATIVE!

LET 'IM GO, PAL, OR YOU'LL SEE WHAT STRONTIUM-90 CAN DO! YOU'LL GET THE MOST INTENSE BLAST OF RADIATION I CAN MUSTER!

I DON'T THINK SO.

NOT WHILE I'M USING YOUR FRIEND AS A SHIELD!

CLEVER BOY.

I'M JUST A LITTLE MORE CLEVER.

WATCH THIS. SINCE THE CURES AND IN-OCULATIONS FOR MOST DISEASES ARE MADE FROM GERMS AND BACILLI... I'M BETTING THAT YOU CAN FORMULATE THE CURE TO WHAT YOU'VE GIVEN ME!

AND YOU'LL DO IT NOW-- OR I'LL SNAP YOU IN HALF!

IT'S... WORKING!

I'VE BECOME... WHOLE!

42

"MY ORIGINS ARE HUMBLE ENOUGH.

"...SO I SPENT MANY HOURS IN THE SHOP, GRINDING EXPERIMENTAL LENSES...

"IN TIMES LIKE THESE, IT'S DIFFICULT STAYING AHEAD OF THE COMPETITION IN ANY BUSINESS...

"...THIS TIME OUT OF A STRANGE MATERIAL I'D RECENTLY DISCOVERED AT A DIG NEAR A TEST SITE."

YOU DON'T WANT TO GIVE THE BAD ELEMENT IN THE NEIGHBORHOOD ANY IDEAS.

"I'D KNOWN THE BEAT COP SINCE I'D OPENED THE STORE...

G'NITE, DOC...

DON'T STAY IN THE STORE TOO LATE.

"...A PATIENT, GENTLE MAN IF EVER I'D MET ONE.

"AT LEAST, THAT'S HOW HE APPEARED THROUGH MY EYES.

"BUT THROUGH MY LENSES..."

"...THAT WAS QUITE SOMETHING ELSE.

"I SAW HIS TRUE NATURE.

"...WHEN I WAS INTERRUPTED BY MY PLEASANT YOUNG ASSISTANT..."

"THE LENSES PIERCED HIS FACADE, ALLOWING ME TO SEE THE TRUTH WITHIN. I CONTINUED TO STARE AFTER HIM, ASTONISHED BY THE REVELATION...

HAVE A NICE EVENING, MR. MEACHAM.

"...A WOMAN WHO, IT SEEMS, WAS STEALING FROM ME TO FEED A VICIOUS DRUG HABIT!

"WHEREVER I TURNED MY ATTENTION, THE LENSES SHOWED ME THE TRUTH.

"HYPOCRISY WAS RAMPANT! I WAS LIVING IN A WORLD OF LIES.

"RESPONDING TO THE MASKS ALL AROUND ME, I MADE ONE OF MY OWN...PLACING LARGER LENSES INSIDE MY HOOD!

"I BECAME MIND'S EYE...THE OMNISCIENT! NO MAN HIDES THE TRUTH FROM ME NOW!"

44

"THE MIND'S EYE STORY PARALLELS MY OWN.

"MY LIFE WAS DEVOTED TO MY WORSHIP. I PRACTICED NIGHTLY WITH MY CHURCH'S CHOIR.

"THE TALL CANDLES ALWAYS HELD A CURIOUS FASCINATION FOR ME.

"...BUT NOW, EVEN MORE SO.

"I SAW A VISION WITHIN ONE.

"A VISION OF AN IDEAL... A VISION OF THE WOMAN I COULD BE-COME THROUGH EVEN STRONGER DEVOTION.

"BUT FIRST, THAT DEVOTION RE-QUIRED A TEST."

BE NOT AFRAID. PLACE YOUR ARM INTO THE FLAME.

"THE FLAMES SPREAD UP MY ARM, ENGULF-ING ALL OF ME...

"UNTIL THE FLAMES AND I WERE ONE. I BECAME VESPER, THE LIVING EMBODIMENT OF SPIRITUALITY AND CANDLELIGHT!"

45

"WE, ON THE OTHER HAND, WERE DEVOTED TO SCIENCE, NOT SPIRITUALITY.

"WE SOUGHT THE SALVATION OF MANKIND THROUGH SCIENTIFIC METHODS... EXPERIMENTING WITH THE EFFECTS OF RADIATION ON DISEASE.

"GERMS APPEARED TO US AS A CODE TRANSMITTED TO THE HUMAN SYSTEM. COULD THEY HAVE AN INTELLIGENCE OF THEIR OWN?

"WE WERE NEVER TO FIND OUT."

GET OUT OF THE WAY! THE BEAM'S ACTIVATED THE BACILLI!

YOW! WHO TURNED ON THE RAY?

I'M COVERED WITH THE STUFF! I COULD BE CONTAMINATED OR... WORSE!

WATCH IT! YOU'VE KNOCKED ME INTO THE BEAM!

"WE WERE CONTAMINATED... BUT ONLY BY POWER!

"THE POWER OF STRONTIUM-90... AND BACILLUS!"

46

CONTINUES NEXT ISSUE...

47

49

50

I CAN SEE WHY D'KAY IS UNIMPRESSED BY HEROES...

...HE MUST BE CREATING SOME OTHER HERO WHO CAN TURN INTO A ROOM DEODORIZER THE SIZE OF MARS.

IS IT *SO* UN-COMFORTABLE HERE FOR YOU, IRON FIST?

YOU'VE BEEN AS GOOD AS *DEAD* BEFORE. SURELY YOU MUST *KNOW* WHAT THIS IS LIKE!

FOR EXAMPLE...

A PLAGUE OF BIBLICAL PROPORTIONS!

SO MANY OF THEM... THE SKY'S ECLIPSED BY THEM ALL! EVERYTHING *AROUND* ME IS BLACK!

THEY'RE... THEY'RE...

EYYYYAAAAAA

MY... MY APOLOGIES, IRON FIST! WE HAVE BEEN... SORELY *DECEIVED!*

D'KAY MEANT ONLY TO GET US INTO THIS TIMELESS DIMENSION... TO *TORTURE* US LIKE MISERABLE *SINNERS!*

TIMELESS, YOU SAY?

THEN THE *HEALING POWER* OF THE *LIVING WEAPON* WILL *WORK* HERE. NO NEED TO WAIT FOR ENOUGH TIME TO PASS... WHERE TIME IS *MEANINGLESS.*

YOU MARSHAL YOUR RESOURCES WELL...

...A REMINDER THAT I HAVE RESOURCES--

--OF MY *OWN.*

I GUESS I NEVER *WAS* REALLY AND TRULY *"DEAD"* BEFORE.

IF I *HAD* BEEN, I WOULD HAVE *REMEMBERED* SOMETHING LIKE *THIS,* THAT'S FOR SURE.

YOU SPEAK TRUTH. AND AS FOR ME-- TO PLACE IT IN WHOLLY EARTHLY TERMS--

--I FEAR THAT I HAVE BEEN *THROWN OUT* OF BETTER PLACES THAN THIS ONE!

HAHAHAHA! YOU *AGREED* TO ACCOMPANY ME TO THE *PIT*. NOW IT IS MEET AND JUST TO FULFILL *MY PART* OF THE *BARGAIN!*

I *DID* HOPE I COULD HAVE TRAPPED YOU HERE, ALLOWING MY HEROES TO GO FORWARD TO SEE MY GRAND SCHEME THROUGH.

BUT HERE OR NOT, YOU'VE BEEN SO INEFFECTUAL AGAINST THE LEGION OF VENGEANCE, THAT IT REALLY DOESN'T MATTER WHETHER YOU FINALLY FACE THEM OR NOT!

EITHER WAY, I WIN!

WIN WHAT? WHAT ARE THE STAKES FOR WHICH YOU GAMBLE?

EVERYTHING. THE ENTIRE POT. I HAVE BET IT ALL ON THESE FOUR AMBITIOUS PEOPLE.

ALL OF THEM COULD SUCCEED IN THEIR OWN FIELDS, BUT THROUGHOUT THEIR PAST LIVES, GREED AND STUPIDITY AND IMPATIENCE MADE THEM PREY TO SIN...

...AND THROUGH SIN I COULD *CONTROL* THEM!

I TOOK OVER THEIR SUBCONSCIOUS MINDS, EACH OF THEM. *TRICKED* THEM INTO BELIEVING THAT THEY WERE *HEROES*. PLANTED RATIONALIZATIONS THAT LED THEM TO BELIEVE THAT ONLY *THEY* WERE *RIGHT* AND *RIGHTEOUS*.

THEY THINK THEY HAVE SUPER POWERS FOR NOBLE, HEROIC REASONS.

BUT THOSE POWERS MAKE THEM MY HARBINGERS OF DOOM!

THEIR EXISTENCE SPELLS NOTHING LESS THAN THE END OF EVERYTHING *HUMAN* ON YOUR WORLD!

AH... A NEW AND SOMBER LOOK OF RESPECT CROSSES YOUR FACES NOW. GOOD... BECAUSE I'D WORRY IF I WERE YOU.

AS MY HARBINGERS OF DOOM, THEY HERALD THE BETRAYAL AND CORRUPTION OF EVERYTHING HUMAN.

AND JUSTICE FOR ALL WHO CAN PAY.

THE MIND'S EYE. HA... THE EYE SEES CLEARLY.: IT IS THE MIND THAT WARPS HIS VISION.

THE MIND THAT ADMINISTERS JUSTICE BASED ON HIS WRONG CONCLUSIONS.

THUS, THE MIND'S EYE IS MY FIRST HERALD OF HUMANITY'S DOOM... THE BETRAYAL OF THE MIND.

AFTER THAT, WHAT ELSE CAN FAIL HUMANITY?

HAVE YOU EVER BEEN SO ILL THAT YOU COULD NOT GET A SINGLE MOTOR NERVE TO OBEY A SIMPLE COMMAND?

THEN YOU HAVE MET MY SECOND HARBINGER OF DOOM... BACILLUS, WHO REPRESENTS THE BETRAYAL OF THE BODY.

DEFILER OF THE ELEMENTS.

DESPOILER OF THE ENVIRONMENT.

SOONER OR LATER, THE VERY PLANET WILL RISE UP AGAINST MANKIND, TO PAY IN KIND THE IRREPARABLE DAMAGE THAT GREED AND STUPIDITY AND IMPATIENCE HAS DONE!

WHEN IT DOES, IT WILL BE LED BY STRONTIUM-90...

...MY AGENT FOR THE BETRAYAL OF THE EARTH.

WHAT IS LEFT FOR MANKIND?

WHEN MIND AND BODY AND EARTH ARE GONE, WHAT FRAGILE HOPE IS THERE LEFT?

LOOK AT HER. SHE COULD GRANT THE MASSES HER GRACE, BUT INSTEAD, SHE USES HER SPIRITUALITY FOR HER OWN GLORIFICATION.

SHE IS THE CORRUPTION OF MAN'S LAST HOPE.

THE AFTERLIFE? GONE. THE SPIRIT? GONE. THE SOUL? GONE.

SHE IS VESPER. SHE IS THE FINAL BETRAYAL. THE BETRAYAL OF GOD.

I CANNOT KEEP YOU HERE. THE GHOST RIDER COULD *EASILY* RETURN YOU TO EARTH FROM THE PIT. SO I CAST YOU BACK.

HERE AND THERE WILL SOON BE *INDIS-TINGUISHABLE* ANYWAY. SO I BID YOU RETURN. YOU WILL SUFFER ...AS *ALL* OF HUMANITY WILL SUFFER!

D'KAY'S SPELL HAS WORN OFF! THE LEGION'S SPRINGING TO *LIFE* AGAIN!

LIFE?

YOU WILL BE NO AUTHORITY ON WHAT CONSTITUTES *LIFE* --

ONCE WE'RE THROUGH!

COURAGE! WE HAVE SEEN THE *END* OF MANKIND, BUT THE END IS NOT YET ...

...FOR IN THE ENDING... I HAVE SEEN THE *SEEDS* OF A NEW BEGINNING!

THE BATTLE IS JOINED!

CONCLUDES NEXT ISSUE.

59

THIS CHAIN CANNOT BE BROKEN... UNLESS I WILL IT!

AND MY WILL...MY RESOLVE....IS STRONGER THAN ANY OF YOURS!

A YANK OF THE CHAIN--

--AND BACILLUS CONTAMINATES *YOU!*

NO!

THE... THE FEVER'S TAKEN ME... ALMOST INSTANTLY!

BACILLUS MUST HAVE BEEN STORING *UP* THAT CHARGE OF CONTAGION FOR SOME TIME...

BUT... HE NEVER MEANT IT TO BE USED ON ME!

VESPER'S BUZZING ME...TAUNTING ME...

...YET STAYING TANTALIZINGLY OUT OF REACH!

IF I COULD JUST GET A CLEAR--

OOG!

HAHAHA!

YOU CAN'T RETALIATE AGAINST AN ADVERSARY YOU CANNOT FIND IN THE DARK!

I'VE GOT A PRETTY GOOD EYE MYSELF!

READY... ...AIM...

...BULLSEYE, SO TO SPEAK!

YOU HAVE MADE THEM A TARGET ...FOR *ME* AS WELL!

BACILLUS'S BOUND HANDS WILL INFECT EACH OF THEM--

--TILL ULTIMATELY, I TURN HIS POWER...ON *HIMSELF!*

YOU WILL SEE THAT WITH FEVER... COMES FEVER *DREAMS.*

THE FEVER WITHIN THEM BURNS BRIGHTER THAN A THOUSAND SUNS!

THEY ARE VULNERABLE ENOUGH NOW FOR US TO *CONTROL* THOSE VISIONS WITH A MERE *SUGGESTION...*

63

THAT'S RIGHT. EVEN *GHOST RIDER*, WHOSE PATH I WOULDN'T WANT TO SHARE, MANAGES TO STEER HIS STRANGE ABILITIES TOWARD THE PATH OF RIGHTEOUSNESS!

SANCTIMONIOUS WORDS...

...BUT THEY RING *HOLLOW!*

BECAUSE I'D NEVER *LET* THAT HAPPEN!

I'LL TAKE THEIR POWERS *AWAY* FIRST!

THERE! THEY'VE BEEN RETURNED TO THEIR HOMES AND LIVES OF OBSCURITY AND MEDIOCRITY! YOU'VE GUARANTEED THAT THEY WILL NEVER KNOW GREATNESS... ONLY *OBLIVION!*

SATISFIED?

I HOPE *THEY* ARE!

THEY ARE BETTER OFF.

I KNOW THAT SUCH POWER IS A *CURSE.*

ONCE YOU GET IT...

...IT'S A BURDEN YOU BEAR THE REST OF YOUR LIFE!

LUST FOR POWER... *ANY* POWER... NEVER FADES!

REST ASSURED... THEY WILL *RETURN!*

HAHAHA!

THE END... FOR NOW!

65

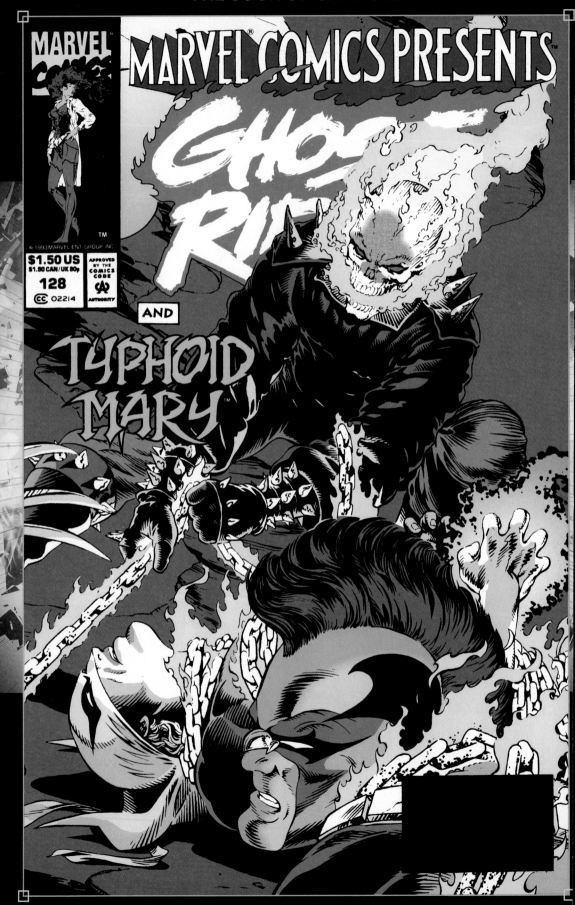

UNDER LOCK AND KEY

THE BOOK OF CHANGES Pt. 1

FEATURING: IRON FIST

AS YOU CAN SEE GENTLE-MEN, RAND'S SECURITY DI-RECTOR COMMANDER MARTINA TERESHKOVA HAS KEPT THE ANOMALY...

GUARDS ARE POSTED TWENTY-FOUR HOURS A DAY IN EIGHT HOUR SHIFTS.

AS TO THE ANOMALY'S *ORIGINS,* IT'S DEFIED X-RAYS, SPECTROSCOPY AND CARBON-DATING.

IT FELLED AN ORACLE WEATHER SATELLITE, BUT WHETHER IT IS IN FACT AN ALIEN ARTIFACT... WE JUST CAN'T TELL.

EYES LEFT, MEN. IF THAT THING GETS STOLEN...

...YOU WOULDN'T WANT IT TO COME OUT OF YOUR PITIFUL PAY-CHECKS.

HMMMMM

WHO'S SHE KIDDIN'? *NOBODY* COULD GET IN HERE.

THIS PLACE COULD HOLD THE *CROWN JEWELS*...EVEN IF THEY WERE RADIOACTIVE!

DR. FARO, WHAT CAUSES THAT INTERMITTENT HUM FROM THE... THE... ANOMALY... AS YOU CALLED IT?

IT'S AS MUCH A MYSTERY AS ANYTHING *ELSE* ABOUT IT...

HMMMMM

A MESSAGE... A SIGNAL, PERHAPS, TO SOMETHING ON THE OUTSIDE.

IF SO, IT'S ATTRACTED NOTHING... *NOTHING* CAN PENETRATE THESE WALLS!

MEN OF SCIENCE ALWAYS REGARD THE WAYS OF THE *OCCULT* AS "NOTHING"...

...TO THEIR EVERLASTING REGRET!

HOW DID *HE* GET IN HERE?

YOU SHOULD INSTEAD ASK--

--WHAT MAKES YOU THINK YOU CAN KEEP OUT...

...*SKELETON KI?!*

OPEN FIRE!

YOU'LL ONLY SUCCEED IN WOUNDING YOURSELVES--

--ONCE THIS SPOILS YOUR AIM.

SO MANY YEARS HAVE PASSED SINCE THE CREATION OF THE COSMIC CUBE.

I REGRET THAT I WASN'T AROUND THEN... TO *STEAL* IT,

BUT *THIS* PRIZE MAY PROVE JUST AS VALUABLE!

71

73

74

76

77

79

"*WHO* TOLD THEM? IT HAD TO BE SOMEONE FROM *INSIDE*.

"I TRAINED MY PROTÉGÉ *RANDY OBERLIN*, IN THE MARTIAL ARTS... WITHOUT THE ARDUOUSNESS OF MY LIFE IN K'UN L'UN. DID *HE* REPAY ME WITH *BETRAYAL?*

"OR DID *DR. FARO* TURN HIS KNOWLEDGE OF THE ANOMALY OVER TO MY ENEMIES?

"*MARTINA TERESHKOVA* IS THE SUPER-EFFICIENT HEAD OF *RAND* SECURITY, BUT IS *SHE* THE SECURITY LEAK?

"*SOMEBODY* BETRAYED *RAND*. WAS IT *ONE* OF THEM?

" OR *ALL* OF THEM?"

I CAN'T TRUST ANYBODY ELSE WITH THIS THING. ONLY I CAN CARRY IT.

CARRY IT **WHERE**?

FAR AWAY FROM **HERE**. THIS COMPOUND HAS BEEN TURNED INTO A **SHAMBLES**.

THE WHOLE **COMPANY** I'VE WORKED SO HARD TO **BUILD** IS A SHAMBLES.

I HAVE ONLY MYSELF TO BLAME. I'VE BEEN "AWAY" TOO LONG, NOT WATCHING THE STORE CAREFULLY ENOUGH. NOW EVERYONE HAS AN AGENDA **OTHER** THAN WORKING FOR ME.

THAT'S **OVER** NOW. I'M GOING "AWAY" FOR **GOOD**.

BUT WHAT ABOUT THE **COMPANY**?

IF YOU WANT, **YOU** MANAGE THE ORGANIZATION. **YOU** DO THE DAMAGE CONTROL.

I DIDN'T GET AN **M.B.A.** IN K'UN L'UN. I'M NOT HERE IN THIS WORLD TO RUN A **CORPORATION**.

I'VE LOST MY SPIRITUAL GUIDES, THE MEN OF K'UN L'UN. NOW I'VE LOST THE WESTERN FAMILY I'VE TRIED TO CREATE.

I USED TO BE **PART** OF THAT FAMILY, YOU KNOW...

ARE YOU SAYING EVEN I DON'T MATTER ANYMORE?

DANIEL? DON'T I MATTER TO YOU?

DANIEL?

DANIEL?

CONTINUES NEXT ISSUE...

82

83

IT RECOGNIZES THE WORLD AS A PLACE OF GREAT BEAUTY... BUT ALSO GREAT *TREACHERY*.

FURTHER, IT REMINDS US THAT *BOTH* THESE QUALITIES EXIST WITHIN OUR *SELVES*.

EACH CANNOT EXIST WITHOUT THE OTHER...

THE LIGHT AND THE DARK...

THE NOBLE AND THE NEEDY...

THE LOYAL AND THE TREACHEROUS...

"...THE YIN AND THE YANG.

"NOT ONLY CAN ONE NOT EXIST WITHOUT THE OTHER...

"...BUT EACH CONTAINS THE QUALITIES OF ITS OPPOSITE.

ZZZZ

"TOO OFTEN, IN WESTERN SOCIETY, WE ENGAGE IN THE *DENIAL* OF THE DARKER SIDE OF OUR BEINGS.

"'OH, NO, NOT ME,' WE SAY. 'I'M A *GOOD* PERSON.'

"'SURELY, THESE DARK DEMONS DO NOT RESIDE WITHIN ME!'

"HOW MUCH BETTER TO RECOGNIZE THEM *NOW,* INSTEAD OF DISCOVERING THE TRUTH WHEN IT IS FAR TOO *LATE.*"

AH, MR. LANDSFIELD... ...I TRUST YOU'VE EXPERIENCED A REVELATION.

HA HA HA

STILL MESSING WITH THEIR MINDS, EH, TOOK?

WHO IS IT THAT STILL KNOWS ME BY THAT UNFORTUNATE SIXTIES APPELATION OF PEREGRIN TOOK?

CAN THAT REALLY BE DANIEL RAND? IF THERE'S *ANYONE* WHO NO LONGER NEEDS A LECTURE FROM ME, IT'S *YOU.*

DON'T BE SO SURE.

85

SO IT'S LIKE THIS, TOOK... MY ENTIRE CORPORATION SEEMS TO HAVE BEEN INFILTRATED BY RIVAL OPERATIVES OF EVERY SORT.

YOU DON'T HAVE TO TELL ME... I KNOW.

YOU KNOW? BUT HOW?

IT ONLY MAKES SENSE. CONSIDER THE YIN-YANG SYMBOL. THE DARK IS INFILTRATED BY THE LIGHT, AND VICE VERSA.

RAND IS A LIGHT SPOT IN A DARKENED WORLD. THESE ENEMY OPERATIVES HAVE BECOME THE DARK SPOT IN AN ENLIGHTENED ORGANIZATION.

TRY SHEDDING SOME ON THIS!

WE ONLY REFER TO IT AS THE ANOMALY... BUT AGENTS OF BOTH AIM AND HYDRA ATTEMPTED TO WREST IT FROM ME.

DANIEL, I KNOW A GREAT MANY THINGS ON A GREAT MANY TOPICS.

YOU COULD ASK ABOUT THE FINE POINTS OF ZOROASTRIAN MYTHOLOGY, VARIETIES OF TIBETAN INCENSE, HOW TO BUILD A TV THAT WATCHES YOU, CHAOS THEORY, OR SEX PISTOLS LYRICS.

THE KEY TO MY KNOWLEDGE IS RESEARCH... AND I NEED A GOOD DEAL MORE OF IT FROM YOUR FIRM BEFORE I COULD BEGIN AN ANALYSIS.

OF COURSE, I DON'T KNOW A SINGLE CONUNDRUM THAT COULDN'T STAND TO BE SOLVED OVER HERBAL TEA.

DANIEL, HAVE YOU MET MY FAVORITE STUDENT, LILLIAN HSU...?

A PLEASURE.

THE PLEASURE... ...IS ALL MINE.

DANIEL, YOU MAY REGARD RECENT EVENTS IN YOUR LIFE AS TREACHERY, BUT I SEE THEM AS AN OPPORTUNITY.

YOU DON'T BELONG IN THE CORPORATE WORLD. IT'S ABOUT TIME YOU DIVESTED YOURSELF OF THIS FIRM THAT'S SPIRALED OUT OF YOUR CONTROL.

WHAT IS YOUR QUEST? TO STAY IN WHO'S WHO... OR THE FORTUNE 500?

YOUR PATH HAS ALWAYS BEEN TO BECOME WHAT THE I CHING CALLS "CHUN-TZU" OR... THE SUPERIOR MAN.

THIS PATH IS A SOLITARY ONE. IT CAN'T BE TROD IF YOU DON'T FREE YOURSELF OF YOUR CORPORATE RESPONSIBILITIES!

GO AWAY AS FAR AS YOU CAN, DANIEL.

EMBARK ON YOUR QUEST ANEW.

87

YOU'RE GONNA BE A PUDDLE.

I DON'T EVEN NEED A GUNSIGHT AT THIS RANGE.

NEITHER DO I.

WITCH. THE PENDANT CAN STOP YOU DEAD, TOO.

NOT YET.

GOOD GOING, LIL.

COVERING THE EYE MEDALLION BROKE THE "SPELL"...

...I'M FREE!

ELSEWHERE...

THERE PROBABLY ISN'T A SINGLE THING ON THIS LOT THAT'S OF ANY USE TO ANYONE ANYMORE...

...UNLESS IT'S MELTED DOWN AS SCRAP METAL.

BUT IF THE *ANOMALY* IS THE NEXT STEP UP IN TECHNOLOGY--

--I'LL FIND OUT WHAT IT DOES... *HERE*, DOWN AMONG DEAD AND DECAYING TECHNOLOGY.

MEANWHILE...

WARRANT'S AN *IDIOT*. WHAT'S THE POINT OF ATTACKING IRON FIST DIRECTLY? THE GUY'S GOT A KARATE CHOP FOR EVERY DAY OF THE WEEK.

WHEN YOUR NAME'S COOL MILLION-- BECAUSE YOU GET A COOL MILLION FOR EVERY GIG-- YOU WORK *SMARTER*, NOT *HARDER*.

NO. THE WAY TO GET TO HIM IS TO GET AT SOMETHING HE CARES ABOUT.

"AND I THINK I'VE FOUND THAT SOMETHING."

CONTINUES NEXT ISSUE...

99

ARE YOU *CRAZY* DRIVING IN HERE LIKE THAT?

I HAVE A *REP* TO UPHOLD. WHAT IF *EVERYBODY* KNEW THAT *THE MECHANIC* WAS IN LEAGUE WITH IRON FIST?

BYE BYE *BUSINESS*.

I *COULD* HAVE LET YOU GO TO *PRISON*, "FRIEND".

HOW MUCH BUSINESS COULD YOU DO FROM THERE?

SO FRIENDSHIP REARS ITS UGLY HEAD.

HMMM... ELECTRON MICROSCOPE REVEALS NOTHING FURTHER...

IT'S RESISTING CHEMICAL ANALYSIS...

...WHAT *IS* THIS PAPERWEIGHT YOU'VE BROUGHT IN?

WOULD IT HELP IF I TOLD YOU THAT THE FORCES OF BOTH *A.I.M.* AND *HYDRA* WANT IT VERY *BADLY*.

OR THAT I'VE BROKEN A FEW OF *MY* FRIENDSHIPS OVER IT AS WELL?

FRIENDS, ALLIANCES COME AND GO. THINGS LIFE THIS GIZMO OCCUR ONCE A *LIFETIME*.

THERE ARE NO FRIENDS I'D *TRUST* WITH THIS...

"...IF ONLY BECAUSE THEY'D ATTRACT MY *ENEMIES.*"

HYDRA WARNED ME THAT IRON FIST MIGHT TAKE THE ANOMALY TO THE *A.I.M.* RENEGADE KNOWN AS *"THE MECHANIC"*...

BUT HE'S NOT LIKELY TO *SURRENDER* THE *ANOMALY* TO ME...

DING DING

...UNLESS I POSSESS A *BARGAINING CHIP.*

YES?

EXCUSE ME, MA'AM. YOU MAY NOT BE AWARE OF THIS...

...BUT THERE'S BEEN A *POISON GAS LEAK* IN THE AREA.

ALL OF YOUR NEIGHBORS--INCLUDING YOURSELF MUST LEAVE THE AREA *IMMEDIATELY.*

MY POWER OF **PERSUASION** WON'T WORK ON **YOU** FROM THIS DISTANCE...

...BUT **THIS** SHOULD **SWAY** THE **DEAL.**

WHOOM

THE CYCLE--!

THUMP

THE MECHANIC'S OUT COLD... AND THE GREAT IRON FIST IS GROGGY ENOUGH FOR ME TO DO **THIS!**

KLAK

A MILLION DOLLARS FOR THIS JOB! **TOO** MUCH, TOO **EASY!**

ONCE MORE, I'VE EARNED MY NICKNAME...

..."COOL MILLION!"

ACGKK!

DON'T CASH THE CHECK YET.

SCREEE

COMPUTER OVERRIDE.

CONTROLS ARE KEYED TO DRIVER'S WEIGHT AND FINGERPRINTS. UNLESS DRIVER IS RE- STORED TO CONTROL...

CAR WILL AUTO- MATICALLY BE SEALED AND DEAD-BOLTED

— AND CAR WILL PROCEED TO PRE-PUNCHED-IN DESTINATION.

THUNK

VROOOOOOOOM

NOT IF I CAN HELP IT!

THE DESTINATION MAY BE PUNCHED IN--

BUT IT'LL SOON BE--

--PUNCHED OUT!

A TRIFLE *LATE* FOR AN ESCAPE ATTEMPT, IRON FIST!

COOL MILLION'S VEHICLE HAS ALREADY ARRIVED IN OUR *MIDST!*

3251

108

110

111

A FORCE BEYOND REASON! A POTENTIAL BEYOND IMAGINING!

UH, SIR? THE ENERGY FEEDBACK FROM THE PYRAMIDS...

...IT LOOKS LIKE IT'S ABOUT TO--

WHAKOOM

IF THAT'S WHAT TWO OF 'EM ARE LIKE, HE BETTER NOT FIND A THIRD ONE!

WHERE DID THE SECOND ANOMALY COME FROM?

MORE IMPORTANT, WHERE IS IT GOING?

IF HE INTENDS TO HARNESS THEIR FORCE AS A WEAPON...

...WE'VE GOT TO FIND SOME WAY TO GET THEM BACK!

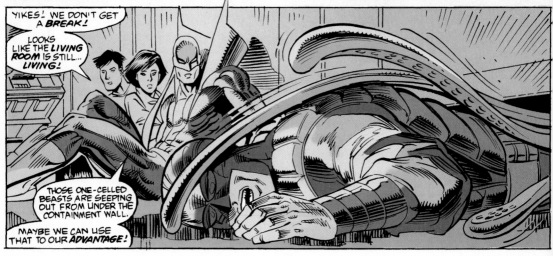

YIKES! WE DON'T GET A BREAK!

LOOKS LIKE THE LIVING ROOM IS STILL... LIVING!

THOSE ONE-CELLED BEASTS ARE SEEPING OUT FROM UNDER THE CONTAINMENT WALL.

MAYBE WE CAN USE THAT TO OUR ADVANTAGE!

A *WEAPON*, IRON FIST? DID I HEAR YOU CORRECTLY?

DO YOU THINK POTENTIAL SUCH AS *THIS* WAS CREATED TO BE A MERE *WEAPON*?

OH, YE OF SCANT *VISION!*

THE FIELD CREATED BY THESE MAGICAL ENTITIES...

...THEY REPRESENT NO LESS THAN THE PORTAL TO ANOTHER *DIMENSION!*

BEHOLD! EVEN *NOW*, THE VISAGE OF SOME OTHERWORLDLY BEING BEGINS TO FORM.

HE'S *RIGHT!*

I CAN'T WAIT TO FIGURE OUT WHICH *SIDE* IT'S GOING TO BE *ON!*

GOT TO USE... ALL MY *STRENGTH*...

...TO *BOOST* THIS *STEEL WALL*...

118

119

THEY MUST OPERATE BY REMOTE CONTROL, BECAUSE THERE'S NO SWITCH NEARBY!

HOW CAN WE TRIP THEM FROM DOWN HERE?

LOAN ME ONE OF THOSE PAPERWEIGHTS,

BE CAREFUL WITH THIS.

RELAX,

...WELL, THEN YOU SHOULD'VE KEPT THE WARRANTY UP TO DATE.

I DON'T MISS.

AND IF I DO....

ZNNG

DID IT! BROKE THE BEAM!

WHIRRR

120

121

--NOW!

THE FRESH AIR FEELS *GOOD.*

ANY SECOND NOW.

THREE-- TWO--

SLAMM

WELL, WHADDAYA KNOW? IT WAS *EARLY.*

WAIT. *THEY* SHOULD HAVE BEEN ABLE TO WORK THE DOOR CONTROL! WHAT *STOPPED* THEM?

THEY SEEM TO HAVE A LIFE OF THEIR OWN!

BUT WHAT'S THEIR SECRET?

WHAT?

IS THIS A CLUE?

NEXT: THE ANSWER AT LAST!

124

THE SUPREME HYDRA WAS **CORRECT**, IRON FIST.

THIS IS INDEED A PORTAL TO ANOTHER DIMENSION.

MY DIMENSION.

I AM KNOWN BY MANY NAMES...TATH KI... MISTER BUDA... THE CONTEMPLATOR.

AND YOUR PURPOSE?

YOU CAME INTO POSSESSION OF WHAT *YOU* HAVE TERMED THE "ANOMALY..."

...BECAUSE IT WAS MY PURPOSE TO SUBVERT *TWO* IMPORTANT EARTHLY ORGANIZATIONS, *HYDRA*...

...AND *RAND* CORPORATION.

I FAILED IN THE FORMER, BUT I SUCCEEDED IN THE LATTER.

BUT WHY? WHY *RAND*?

FOR YOUR OWN SAKE, FOR OUR OWN PEACE AND CONTENTMENT.

HYDRA IS BEYOND REDEMPTION... BEYOND MY POWER TO DISBAND OR REVERT IT.

BUT TO BRING PEACE AND CONTENTMENT TO YOUR TROUBLED SOUL, *RAND* HAD TO LOSE ITS GUIDING SPIRIT... *YOU.*

YOUR FAITH HAS BEEN SHAKEN BY THE *CORRUPTION* THAT PERVADES *RAND.* SOMEONE HAS *BETRAYED* YOU WITH-IN ITS RANKS... AND THIS HAS HURT YOU DEEPLY.

WHO WAS IT? FARO? TERESHKOVA? OBERLIN?

TELL ME! *WHO?*

I CANNOT. I *WILL* NOT.

YOU HAVE LEFT THAT ORGANIZATION BEHIND. SO SHALL IT BE.

THE ANSWER SHOULD NO LONGER MATTER TO YOU. YOU MUST TRANSCEND IT.

YOU SHOULD BECOME BEYOND *CARING* IF YOU ARE TO EMBARK ON A NEW QUEST-- A QUEST TO BECOME THE *SUPERIOR MAN.*

126

127

...FOR YOUR QUEST IS NOT MERELY TO BECOME THE SUPERIOR MAN...

... TO ATTAIN PERFECTION FOR YOURSELVES...

...BUT TO HELP OTHER HUMANS TO ATTAIN A GOAL THAT IS UNREACHABLE... UNATTAINABLE!

THE GOAL OF...

...UNIVERSAL PERFECTION.

THAT SAID, NOT ALL OF YOUR DEALINGS ON YOUR QUEST WILL BE ON SUCH A RARIFIED, COSMIC PLANE.

I HAVE MADE YOU READY TO DEAL ONCE AGAIN WITH THE *LOWLIFE*...

...BUT UNDERSTAND...

...I AM ALWAYS WITH YOU.

AS EASILY AS I FUSE BOTH THESE POWERFUL DIMENSIONAL CONDUITS TOGETHER...

...YOU CAN USE THE RESULT OF THAT BONDING TO *SUMMON* ME.

IT IS YOURS. IT IS YOUR ORACLE, YOUR SPIRITUAL COMPASS TO CONSULT FOR DIRECTION, AS HUMANS FOR AGES HAVE CONSULTED THE BOOK OF CHANGE.

YOU LITERALLY NOW HAVE THE FUTURE IN YOUR HANDS, IRON FIST.

YOU HAVE BEEN GIVEN A *LIGHT. USE* IT TO GUIDE HUMANITY OUT OF THE TUNNEL.

SO YOU'RE SAYING EVERY-THING *ELSE* IS *JUST* A LIGHT?

WHATEVER LIES AHEAD...

...I'M *READY*.

NEVER THE END.

NAMOR THE SUB-MARINER ANNUAL #3 PINUP BY JAE LEE

GREATER EVIL

Featuring IRON FIST

THE HIMALAYAS...

"ROOF OF THE WORLD", THEY CALL IT.

MOST OF THIS "ROOF" STARTS AT FIFTEEN THOUSAND FEET ABOVE SEA LEVEL. GO HIGHER AND THE SNOW'S SO DEEP IT NEVER MELTS, SO WHITE IT BLINDS A MAN. IN A FEW HOURS, FROSTBITE'S A GIVEN.

IT'S ONE OF THE MOST BEAUTIFUL PLACES I'VE EVER BEEN.

RON MARZ--WRITER
ANDY SMITH--BREAKDOWNS
BRAD VANCATA--FINISHES/COLORS
UL HIGGINS--LETTERER
TERRY KAVANAGH--EDITOR
TOM DEFALCO--CHIEF

I FIRST VISITED **TIBET** YEARS AGO. I SUPPOSE, LIKE **MOST** WESTERNERS, I CAME **SEARCHING** FOR SOMETHING.

I FOUND **FRIENDS**.

NOW, YEARS LATER...

...I'M **SEARCHING** FOR THEM AGAIN.

...IRON FIST... YOU CAME...

LHOSANG!

...YOU... GOT OUR **MESSAGE**... YOU CAME...

OF COURSE, LHOSANG. BUT IT TOOK SO LONG TO *REACH* ME... BY *THAT* TIME THE MESSAGE WAS IN-COMPLETE.

IT SAID THERE WAS A *THREAT* TO THE MONASTERY. *WHO? THE CHINESE?*

THEY CAME... CAME WITH *GUNS*... TOLD US TO LEAVE, TO *CLOSE* DREPLING MONASTERY...

WE *WAITED* FOR YOU... TO SAVE US... BUT YOU DID NOT COME.

WE HAD NO CHOICE... BUT TO SUMMON...

...SUMMON...

LHOSANG!

LHOSANG!

SAVE OUR HOLY MONASTERY! YOU *MUST!* SEE THAT IT IS NOT *DEFILED!*

HE *DIED* A MOMENT LATER. LHOSANG WAS ONE OF THE *NOBLEST* MEN I'D EVER MET.

ALL I COULD DO FOR HIM WAS *BURY* HIS BODY IN A SNOW DRIFT.

THAT... AND *CARRY OUT* HIS DYING REQUEST.

TIBETAN CULTURE USED TO BE WHOLLY DICTATED BY *RELIGION*. BUDDHIST MONASTERIES WERE THE *CENTER* OF LIFE.

UNTIL *MAO* SENT HIS RED ARMY INTO TIBET IN 1950 UNDER THE GUISE OF *LIBERATING* AN OPPRESSED PEOPLE. THE ENSUING *PURGE* BY THE CHINESE WAS DESIGNED TO *ELIMINATE* TIBET'S IDENTITY, MORE THAN TWO HUNDRED THOUSAND DIED IN A FAILED CULTURAL REVOLUTION.

CHINA STILL *CONTROLS* TIBET. BUT DESPITE THE *BEST EFFORTS* OF THE CHINESE, MONASTERIES LIKE DREPLING *MAINTAIN* THE BUDDHIST TRADITIONS. RELIGIOUS ORDERS AND THE MILITARY *CLASH* REGULARLY.

SOMETIMES IT TURNS *VIOLENT*.

BOTH SOLDIERS AND MONKS *DEAD*, TORN APART.

WHAT *HAPPENED* HERE?

WHAT COULD HAVE *DONE* THIS?

135

IT'S AN ACT OF SACRILEGE.

THE ORNATE LABOR OF CENTURIES, ALL BROUGHT DOWN IN A MOMENT OF SPLINTERING TIMBER AND CASCADING SNOW.

BUT ULTIMATELY THERE WAS NO OTHER CHOICE.

IN ORDER TO PRESERVE THIS SHRINE...

I AM FORCED TO DESTROY IT.

END.

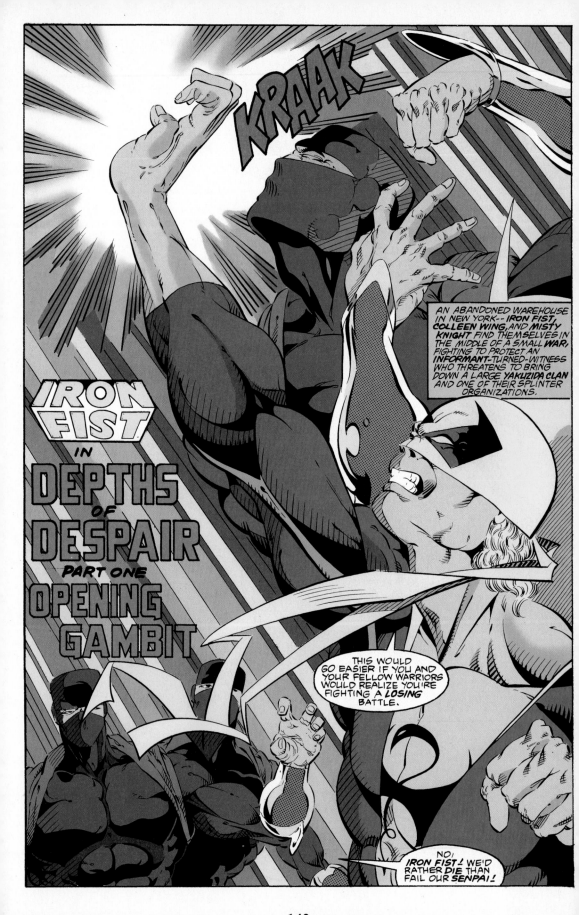

143

THE HEADQUARTERS OF THE **YAKUZIDA**, LOCATED NOT TOO FAR FROM WHERE THE BATTLE WAGES...

A PRIVATE COMPLEX, KNOWN ONLY TO A FEW-- ITS OUTER FACADE BELIES ITS TRUE NATURE... THE QUIET SERENITY, A DECEPTION.

THEIR LEADER, **MR. SHIRO** IS FURIOUS OVER A SMALL FACTION OF HIS RED DRAGONS BREAKING AWAY AND CREATING THEIR OWN "TONGS".

AAAHH... I'M GLAD YOU'RE **FINALLY** HERE. I'VE NEVER BEEN ONE TO TOLERATE LATENESS. NOW, COME IN-- WE NEED TO SPEAK.

DO YOU ALWAYS TALK THIS WAY TO YOUR EMPLOYEES? OR ARE YOU JUST HAPPY TO SEE ME?

YOUR WIT AND CHARMING PERSONALITY ARE, AS EVER, ASTOUNDING.

WELL, I'M FUN AT PARTIES, TOO.

I HAVE LOST MY PATIENCE. I WANT THIS DONE QUICKLY, AND CLEAN.

SOME OF MY MEN WILL ACCOMPANY YOU. I, FOR ONE, DO NOT TRUST YOUR SUPPOSED PROWESS ...YOU ARE NOTHING BUT AN **ANIMAL.**

THE WAY I FIGURE IT IS THAT YOU'RE NOT LONG FOR THIS WORLD, SO, I'LL KILL THIS POWERS INFORMANT GUY...

...AND FOR NO EXTRA CHARGE, I'LL DO YOU. SOUND GOOD.

NO, **SABRETOOTH,** IT DOES NOT. JUST KILL HIM.

SNARRL

MEANWHILE, THE SITUATION IN THE NEARBY WAREHOUSE GROWS GRIM....

KRAAK

DANNY! HE MUST BE HURT...HIS MOVES ARE SO STIFF.

FIST'S REACTIONS ARE SLOWER, HIS MOVES ARE TOO *DEFENSIVE* TO BE EFFECTIVE...HE HAS TO PRESS THE ATTACK.

KWAP

HOW CAN YOU CALL YOURSELF A WARRIOR WHEN YOU LACK A KILLING STYLE

THE GREAT *IRON FIST*-- *HAH!* YOU FIGHT WITHOUT GRACE OR PASSION. YOUR *CHI* IS SOFT.

HE'S RIGHT! MY MOVES--AND MINDSET--ARE WEAK. I CAN'T APPLY MYSELF EFFECTIVELY.

A WARRIOR DOES NOT ALLOW HIMSELF TO BE DISTRACTED.

HIS MIND SHOULD BE UNCLUTTERED... CLEARLY YOURS IS NOT.

WHAT'S WRONG WITH FIST? HE'S GETTING HIS BUTT HANDED TO HIM.

COLLEEN! HURRY, WE HAVE TO HELP HIM.

YOU'RE BLINDED BY YOUR OWN RAGE. OPEN YOUR EYES. YOU'RE BEING USED BY YOUR SENPAI, JUST LIKE SHIRO WAS USING YOU.

YOU BROKE OFF FROM YOUR FAMILY, FOR WHAT? DRUGS, WEAPONS, PROSTITUTION, AND ASSASSINATIONS? WHERE IS THE HONOR IN THAT?

WE WANTED OUR FREEDOM. WE FIGHT FOR US, NOT SOMEONE ELSE... WE'RE UNITED NOW.

POWERS WAS PART OF YOUR "UNITED" GROUP UNTIL HE FINALLY REALIZED IT WAS ONLY A MATTER OF TIME BEFORE HE WAS KILLED.

JOIN ME AND MY FRIENDS... FIGHT WITH US... HELP US BRING SHIRO TO JUSTICE.

YOUR BRAND OF JUSTICE, ONE THAT WE DO NOT BELIEVE IN.

HONOR AND JUSTICE ARE TO BE FOUND IN COMBAT.

THAT IS WHY YOU ARE INHERENTLY FLAWED... YOU FIGHT A HOLLOW BATTLE.

KLAK

YOU FIGHT LIKE A BEATEN MAN. ONLY YOU DON'T KNOW IT YET. YOU ARE SO LOST WITHIN YOURSELF, YOU NO LONGER HAVE THE SPIRIT TO FIGHT. YOUR VISION IS CLOUDED... YOU CAN NO LONGER SEE THE TRUTH.

NO!

WE HAVE TO HELP HIM, COLLEEN!

NO, MISTY! DANNY HAS TO DO THIS BY HIMSELF. IF WE HELP HIM, HE'LL CONTINUE TO DOUBT HIMSELF, AND TO HIM, THAT'S WORSE THAN DEATH. LET HIM GO, HE'LL BE FINE...

...I HOPE.

147

CLOUDED? NO... I MIGHT NOT BE THE SAME MAN SINCE "RETURNING FROM THE DEAD"*, BUT I AM STILL A WARRIOR.

I WILL NOT STAND QUIETLY BY AND LET AN INNOCENT MAN BE MURDERED, BE- CAUSE YOU HAPPEN TO HAVE A DEMENTED VIEW OF LIFE AND JUSTICE.

*NAMOR #23.--Terry

YOU TAKE YOUR SKILLS AND TRAINING, AND OFFER IT TO ANYONE. YET YOU ARE NOT AFRAID TO ACCEPT WEAKNESS. I WILL WORK UNTIL THEY ARE NO LONGER MY FAULTS, BUT MY STRENGTHS. CAN YOU SAY THE SAME?

I HAVE SEEN AND EXPERIENCED MUCH VIOLENCE, ENDURED PAIN AND LEARNED FROM IT. THAT IS THE REASON I AM THE MAN THAT I AM.

THAT IS WHY I NEVER LOSE. I WILL ALWAYS FIND A WAY TO WIN... AND RAISE MYSELF ABOVE THOSE WHO CAN'T.

YOU CAN SAY THE SAME?

SKRAASH

148

CAN YOU? WHERE IS YOUR BRAVADO NOW, WARRIOR? I COULD TAKE YOUR LIFE WITH ONE BLOW... BUT I WILL NOT.

IT IS HARDER TO ACCEPT YOUR ENEMY THAN IT IS TO KILL THEM.

I AM NO MURDERER. YET I WILL DEFEAT YOUR CLAN... AND *ANYONE* THAT TRIES TO HARM AN INNOCENT.

TELL THEM TO COME. *I'LL BE WAITING.*

P L O P

A QUIET EVENING, HE HEARS THE VIOLENCE, SMELLS THE ANGER AND THE SWEAT... IT'S EXHILARATING. HE IS ENTHRALLED BY THE EMOTIONS... THRIVES ON THEM.

HE JUMPS FROM ROOF-TOP TO ROOF-TOP AS EASILY AS ANOTHER MAN WOULD TAKE A STEP.

AAAHH... LOVE THE *SMELL OF BLOOD.*

AND BEFORE THE NIGHT'S OVER, IT'LL FLOW IN RIVERS THROUGH THE STREETS.

HA HA HA HA HA!

CONTINUES NEXT ISSUE...

149

COLLEEN--MY... A BIT MELODRAMATIC, ARE WE?

I AM AMAZED AT YOUR ARROGANCE. BUT IT WILL MAKE IT A GREATER PLEASURE TO KILL YOU AND YOUR FRIENDS.

THEN WE WILL ELIMINATE KARL POWERS -- THE TURNCOAT INFORMANT-- AND REJOICE IN OUR VICTORY!

OOOFF!

CRAAK

THE ONLY THING YOU'LL EXPERIENCE WILL BE COLD STEEL THROUGH YOUR HEART!

AAIEEE!

IT SEEMS YOUR BATTLE PROWESS IS NOT AS IM-PRESSIVE AS YOU WOULD LIKE TO BELIEVE.

CRACK

HHH!

MISSED!

MEANWHILE... IN ANOTHER SECTION OF THE WAREHOUSE, WHERE THE F.B.I. IS PROTECT-ING THE INFORMANT.

CLICK

THOUGHT I HEARD SOMETHIN'...

GETTIN' WHAT YOU WANT, MIGHT BE WORSE THAN NOT.

DITTO ON THAT. THE QUIETER, THE BETTER.

BE CAREFUL WHAT YOU WISH FOR...

I HATE THIS WAITING. I HOPE SOMETHING HAPPENS SOON.

152

153

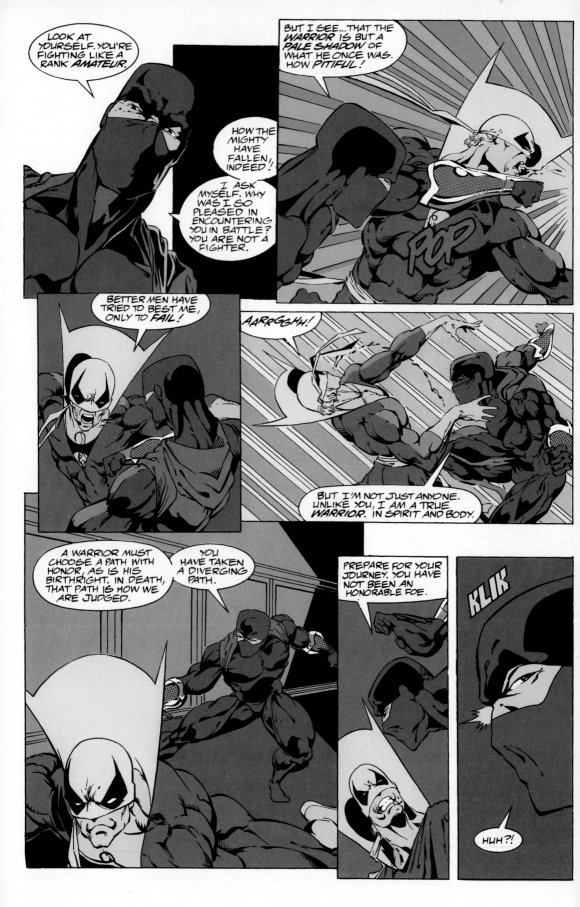

154

14

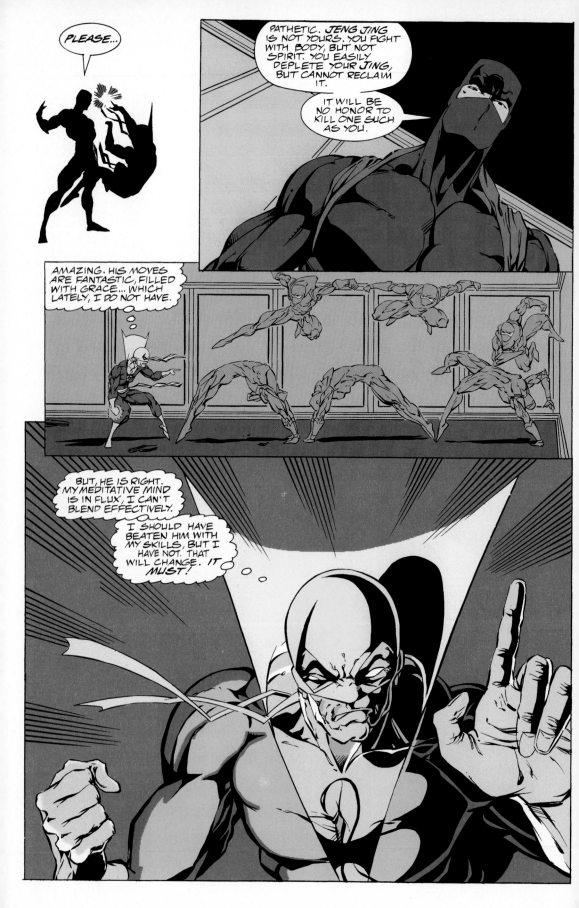

156

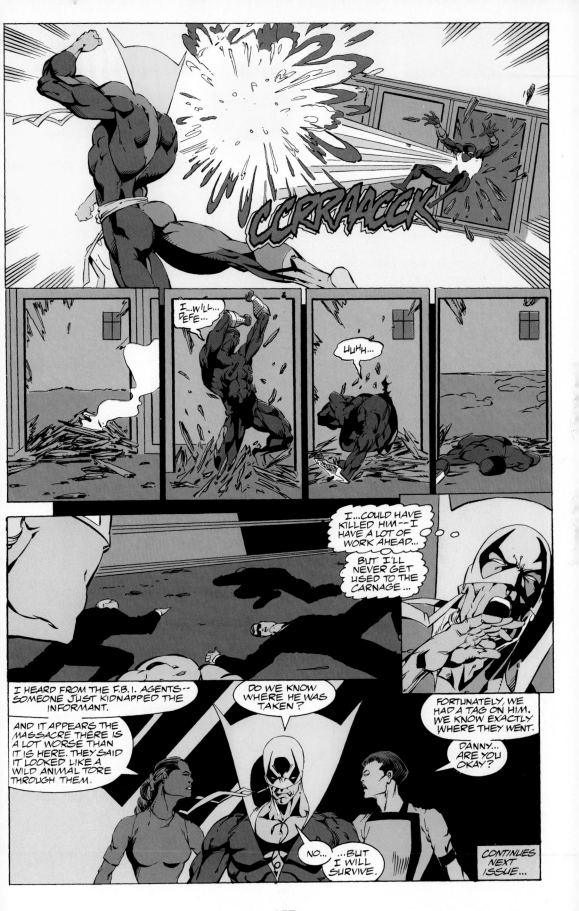

BACK AND FORWARD

I'M STILL ANGRY AT MYSELF FOR LETTING THE DRAGONS *TAKE CARL POWERS* FROM US.

BUT NOW THAT THEY THE INFORMANT, THEY WILL MOST LIKELY KILL HIM, AND THEY WILL EXPAND THEIR ILLEGAL BUSINESSES UNCHECKED THROUGH- OUT THE CITY.

YOU MAKE IT SOUND AS THOUGH WE'VE LOST ALREADY, DANNY... BUT I'M NOT ONE TO GIVE UP. AND NEITHER ARE YOU.

I JUST WISH THAT THEY HAD DECIDED TO HOLE UP SOMEWHERE ELSE... MAYBE THE RAMADA.

AHHH... COLLEEN-- YOU KNOW ME WELL.

WELL, *IRON FIST*--ANY- THING YET...?

NO...BUT I HAVE A FEELING THAT THEY ARE VERY--

PLIK

--CLOSE?

158

KRASH

DEATH TO ALL WHO OPPOSE US.

THE YOUNG WARRIOR IS MINE.

HERE WE GO AGAIN.

THE *DRAGONS* ARE NOTHING IF NOT PERSISTENT.

WE MUST BE GETTING CLOSE TO THEIR BASE OF OPERATIONS. OUR *F.B.I.* TAIL WAS RIGHT--THEY DUCKED INTO THESE TUNNELS. IT'S ONLY A MATTER OF TIME BEFORE WE GET TO POWERS

I WISH I FELT AS CONFIDENT AS I SOUND.

MISTY! COLLEEN! SPREAD OUT AND START LOOKING FOR THE INFORMANT. *I'LL* HANDLE THE DRAGON WARRIORS.

UUHH!

THESE CULTISTS ARE GETTING INCREASINGLY HARDER TO DEFEAT. THEIR TECHNIQUES ARE *INCREDIBLE*-- THEY'RE WELL-TRAINED AND DISCIPLINED.

WAIT! THEY'RE BACKING OFF-- NO LONGER CONCERNING THEM- SELVES WITH ME. SOMETHING ELSE... CONCENTRATE. DON'T LET YOUR GUARD DOWN...

AAAARRGGHH!

$%0&*! SABRETOOTH-- OUT OF NOWHERE...

RRIPP

WELL, IF IT ISN'T MY OLD BUDDY, IRON FIST.

I'M SORRY... -:ACK:... HE WAS TOO FAST.

SHUT UP!

YOU BOYS TAKE CARE OF THE RAT FOR A WHILE--IT'S TIME TO SLICE AND DICE.

LOOKS LIKE MR. LIVING WEAPON HAS LOST HIS EDGE.

WELL, FIST, YOU KNOW WHY I HAVEN'T KILLED HIM YET? I WANTED TO DO IT IN FRONT OF YOU--SO YOU CAN SEE YER FAILURE TO PROTECT HIM UP CLOSE AND PERSONAL!

SHEESH. I KNOW YOU'VE SEEN BETTER DAYS, CHUMP. WHAT'S THE MATTER, OLD AGE CATCHIN' UP TO YOU...?

I'M LUCKY SABRETOOTH HASN'T KILLED ME YET--GUESS MY ACE IN THE HOLE IS HOLDING UP. I HOPE THAT IRON FIST IS AS GOOD AS THEY SAY HE IS, OR I MIGHT STILL END UP DEAD.

SPLASH

NOT SABRETOOTH. I'M NOT READY FOR HIM YET.

COLLEEN, BE HONEST. ISN'T THIS SCENE GETTING TIRED.

YEAH. LET'S END THIS QUICK.

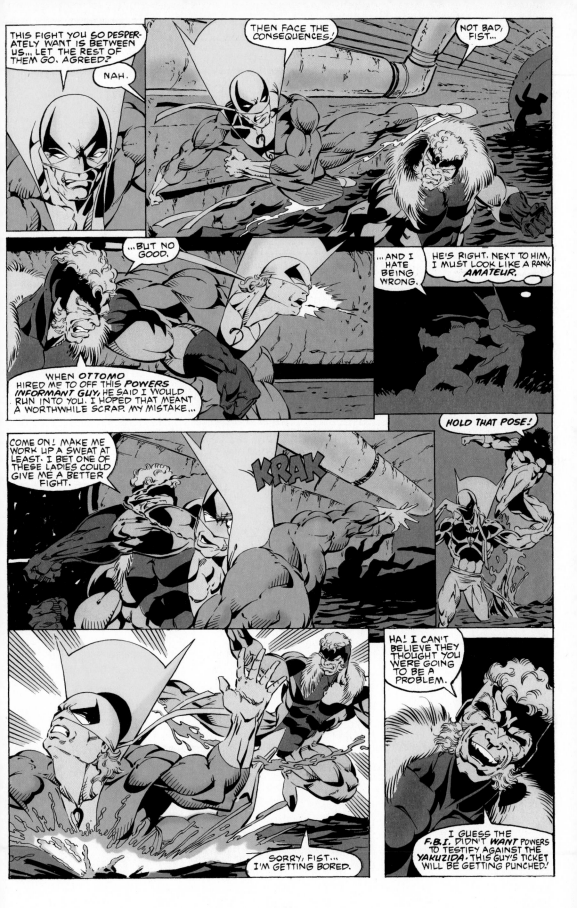

161

BLAM BLAM BLAM

DANNY! I HAVE TO HELP DANNY SOMEHOW!

COLLEEN... COVER ME. I'M GOING TO TRY TO HELP. MY BIONIC ARM MAY BE ABLE TO PETER THEM MORE THAN MY .357.

MISTY... UHH, I BEG TO DIFFER.

WHAT?

WHAT IS IT WITH THESE GUYS? DO THEY COME WITH A WARRANTY, OR WHAT?

I REALLY HOPE YOU HAVE MORE AMMO, MISTY--

HUH! TOO QUICK-- ≷UHF≷

COLLEEN!

YOU SHOULD HAVE STAYED AWAY. BY FOLLOWING US, YOU HAVE SIGNED YOUR OWN DEATH WARRANTS.

STOP! BACK OFF... SLOWLY.

SPARE ME YOUR THEATRICS. YOUR JOHN WAYNE IS LONG DEAD.

WELL, YOU CAN JOIN HIM.

KLIK

VERY IMPRESSIVE.

EMPTY! OH, $*&#@!

YOU HAVE BREATHED YOUR LAST BREATH, WOMAN-- PREPARE TO DIE.

DROP HER!

LISTEN TO ME. KARL POWERS IS OF NO VALUE TO US ANYMORE. THE INFORMATION THAT HE WOULD GIVE TO YOU NO LONGER APPLIES TO US.

WE REALIZED THAT IT WOULD BETTER SERVE US IF WE SHIFTED OUR ATTENTION ELSEWHERE. SO, BY ALL MEANS, KEEP HIM... WE'LL BE LEAVING.

UUUUH... CAN WE DISCUSS THIS?

SPOP

WHO?! WAIT! SHE'S SHE.

THEY'RE BOWING! SHE MUST BE THE LEADER OF THE DRAGONS!

LEAVE! THE MISSION HAS BEEN TERMINATED. RETURN TO BASE-- I'LL DEAL WITH THE WOMEN.

YES, SENPAI!

IRON FIST HAS BEEN IN MANY BATTLES, ALWAYS CONFIDENT THAT HE WOULD BE THE VICTOR. NOW, FOR THE FIRST TIME, HE IS UNSURE.

HE REALIZES THAT TO GO FORWARD, ONE MUST SOMETIMES RELIVE THE PAST.

HE NEEDS TO TAKE A STEP *BACK* IN ORDER TO WALK FORWARD--

-- SHUT OFF ALL THE SENSES EXPERIENCING NOTHING, TO CRAWL INTO A SELF-CREATED GRAVE. *TO BE REBORN,* AND EMERGE ONCE AGAIN.

FINE, SABRETOOTH--IF IT'S A FIGHT YOU WANT, I'LL GIVE YOU ONE YOU WON'T SOON FORGET.

YEAH, RIGHT.

I'M GOING TO RIP YOUR HEART OUT AND HOLD IT UP TO YOUR DYING EYES.

I MUST FORGET ALL THAT HAS HAPPENED. REMEMBER WHAT I AM-- THIS DAY SABRETOOTH WILL *FALL!*

GET READY, SPORT... I'M GOING TO SEPARATE YOUR BREATH FROM YOUR BODY, AND ALL YOUR CARES WILL SOON BE FORGOTTEN!

CONCLUDES NEXT ISSUE...

165

BACK TO THE BEGINNING

IRON FIST, COLLEEN WING and MISTY KNIGHT HAVE BEEN RECRUITED BY THE F.B.I. TO HELP THEM PROTECT FORMER RED DRAGON TURNED F.B.I. INFORMANT KARL POWERS.

THEIR MISSION: BRING DOWN A RENEGADE FACTION OF THE RED DRAGONS.

IRON FIST

MEANWHILE, SABRETOOTH, WORKING FOR THE ORIGINAL TONG FACTION, IS SENT TO ELIMINATE POWERS, AND THE RENEGADE FACTION OF RED DRAGONS.

COME ON, FIST. LET'S PUT ON A LITTLE DANCE FOR OUR FRIENDS HERE. I KNOW YOU WON'T DISAPPOINT ME. RIGHT?

WE SHALL SEE. IT SEEMS THAT THOSE WHO ARE FILLED WITH BRAVADO ARE THOSE WHO ARE UNSURE OF THEMSELVES.

YEAH RIGHT. WHO'S LOSIN' THIS FIGHT? GET REAL, CHUMP!

167

WELL, AREN'T WE THE CONFIDENT ONE WHERE DID YOU GET THE SUDDEN MAN-HOOD?

LISTENING TO YOUR RATTLING IS ALL I NEED. I'VE DECIDED TO PERSONALLY SHUT YOU UP.

OOOH. I'M SHAKIN' IN MY BOOTS.

IRON FIST.

WHY ARE YOU STILL HERE? GET OUT!!

WHAT I'M GOING TO DO NEXT IS DANGEROUS. I DON'T WANT THEM NEAR.

TURN AROUND, FIST.

SURE.

I MAY NOT HAVE THE POWER OF IRON FIST BUT I CAN STILL SUMMON UP MY CHI!

I'M A WARRIOR, NO ONE WILL DEFEAT ME. NO MATTER WHAT CONDITION I MIGHT BE IN. I WILL ALWAYS WIN. ALWAYS.

AAARRGH!

KRAPOW

KRACKLE

KRACKLE

KRASH

LUCKY WE WERE CLOSE TO A SERVICE EXIT!

FREE!

UUH...

FIST! ARE YOU OKAY?

NO, BUT I GUESS I'LL LIVE.

THANK GOD, YOU WERE ABLE TO USE YOUR IRON FIST TO PUNCH THE FALLING DEBRIS. I'M SURE MY BIONIC ARM COULDN'T DO IT.

WELL... THAT'S WHY YOU KEEP ME... OUCH...MY RIBS... AROUND.

YEAH. WHO NEEDS THE BORING LIFE? RIGHT? WELL... WE WON...

HA HA HA

TINK

KRACK

KRASH

THE END?

177

...MEANING YOU'VE GOT A *PASSENGER!*

A DROLL TURN OF PHRASE. PERHAPS I CAN MAKE A GENTLEMAN OF YOU AFTER ALL... INSTEAD OF SHAKING YOU LOOSE, TO PLUMMET FIFTY STORIES!

YOU *CAN'T.* I'M NAMED *IRON FIST* FOR A *REASON.*

THE SITUATION IS ALWAYS WELL WITHIN MY *TIGHT GRASP!*

SO YOU SAY. HOWEVER...

...THE HIGHWAYMAN ALWAYS HAS A TRICK OR TWO UP HIS SLEEVE!

LIKE A LASER PISTOL THAT CAN SLICE YOU AS EASILY...

...AS A HOT BLADE THROUGH THE NECK OF A CHRISTMAS GOOSE!

A COOKED GOOSE, I HASTEN TO POINT OUT!

178

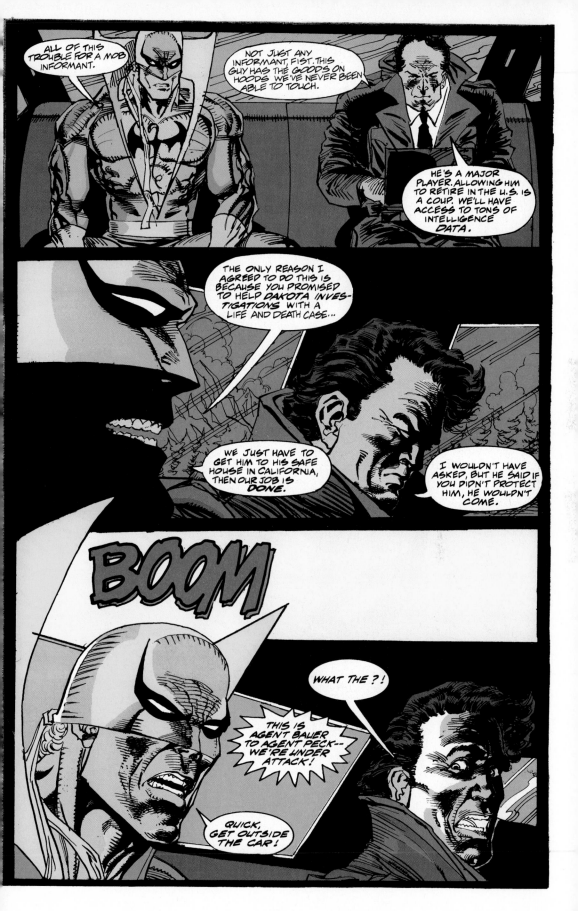

183

185

186

189

195

197

AFTER-HOURS IN THE MORGUE...

...OF NEW YORK'S DAILY BUGLE BUILDING.

TECHNICALLY, THIS IS REALLY NONE OF *PETER PARKER'S* BUSINESS.

BUT THE STREET RUMORS ABOUT *A.R.M.S.*-- *ALTERNATIVE RESOURCES MUNITIONS SUPPLY*-- INDICATE AN AGGRESSIVE *PUBLIC STRIKE* OF SOME SORT SOON...

...TO *LAUNCH* THEIR *MYSTERIOUS NEW PRODUCT* INTO THE *UNDERGROUND WEAPONS MARKET* TRADITIONALLY MONOPOLIZED BY *A.I.M.**

*ADVANCED IDEA MECHANICS. --DANNY

AND THAT'S *BOUND* TO BECOME *SPIDER-MAN'S* BUSINESS.

"*FILES* I 'BORROWED' FROM KATE CUSHING'S INVESTIGATION POINTED ME TO THIS PAPER TRAIL OF *LEGAL WEAPONS SHIPMENTS* AND A *SUSPICIOUS PURCHASE OF TITANIUM...*"

RAND RESCUES WOBBLY WEAPONS WAREHOUSES

After losing their most lucrative government contracts under the new administration's reduced defense budget, two local munitions manufacturer's were saved from bankruptcy by inventory sales to Rand Research and Development in (continues next page)

RAND DIPS INTO TITANIUM MARKET

Rand Research and Development's unprecedented purchase of a large quantity of Titanium from Titan, Inc. has reversed the downward trend of their stock (continues on page b-4)

"...THAT *STOPS DEAD* ON THIS PARTICULAR CORPORATE DOORSTEP."

RAND DIPS INTO T
Rand Research a
quantity of Titaniu

SOON AS THE HARD COPY'S *PRINTED OUT,* I CAN--

BZZZ

PETER, DOWN TO THE CITY ROOM ON THE *DOUBLE!*

AHH...THE EVER-GLAMOROUS LIFE OF A FREELANCE PHOTOGRAPHER FOR AN INTREPID DAILY NEWSPAPER--

"--ALWAYS ON CALL."

KLK

KLK

TEK

"NO WAY TO KNOW IF THIS IS EVERYTHING THE BUGLE HAS GATHERED ON A.R.M.S...."

...BUT I HEAR THE GUY RETURNING SOONER THAN ANTICIPATED.

ALTHOUGH I WOULD HAVE PREFERRED TO AVOID THIS...

Stan Lee presents:
SPIDER-MAN
in
"STORM WARNINGS"
PART ONE
...IRON FIST MUST NOT BE TRAPPED AGAIN!
TERRY KAVANAGH, WRITER
JAE LEE, ARTIST
KEVIN TINSLEY, COLORIST
JOE ROSEN, LETTERER
DANNY FINGEROTH, EDITOR
TOM DeFALCO, EDITOR IN CHIEF

WHAT THE...?!

SPIDER-SENSE DIDN'T WARN ME OF ANY DANGER--

--AND THE ATTACKER LEFT MORE THAN ENOUGH CASH TO COVER THE DAMAGE TO THE WALL--

--BUT SOMEBODY DID A VERY UNCOOL THING.

EXPLAINS WHY I WAS LURED OUT OF THE ROOM BY AN EXCELLENT IMPRESSION OF THE VACATIONING JOE ROBERTSON...

PURGE

...AND IT LOOKS LIKE OUR UNINVITED VISITOR WENT THIS-A-WAY--

--UNTIL MAKING A MAJOR LEAP TO THE NEAREST ROOF.

BUT WHOEVER IT WAS IS ALSO FAST ENOUGH TO BE LONG GONE ALREADY...

"...LEAVING ME IN DEEP TROUBLE."

BRNNG

KATE...?

MS. CUSHING TO YOU AT THIS HOUR OF THE NIGHT, PARKER...

...WHAT'S THE PROBLEM?

ABOUT YOUR A.R.M.S. STORY-FILES...

OFF LIMITS, MISTER! I HAVEN'T EVEN HAD A CHANCE TO BACK-UP THOSE DISCS...

"...YOU TOUCH THEM AND I'LL HAVE YOUR JOB!"

"AERIAL SECURITY CAMERAS COVERED WITH WEBBING...

SHIFTING SHADOWS THROUGH THE SKYLIGHT...

SPIDER-MAN IS ON THE ROOF.

FIND: RAND RESEARCH. SEARCHING...

"FAINT VIBRATIONS FROM THE CEILING...

CAMERA 007   CAMERA 008

BUT THE TECHNOLOGY OF DANIEL RAND AND THE DISCIPLINES OF IRON FIST BOTH REQUIRE TIME TO CHART THE PATH OF DECEIT THROUGH THIS RAW DATA...

...AND SPIDER-MAN MERELY STUDIES ME AS I CONTEMPLATE THE NEWLY ACQUIRED DOCUMENTATION.

SO I HAVE NO CAUSE TO ACT UNTIL HE MAKES--

RAND RESEARCH-Personnel

207

-- IRON FIST HAS GONE ROGUE!

BELIEVE WHAT YOU WILL, FRIEND...

WHFF

"...I HAVE REASON TO KEEP YOU IN THE DARK."

...BY THE TIME MY SPIDER-SENSE RESPONDS TO ONE THREAT FROM THE SHADOWS--

KICKING OUT THE LIGHTS GIVES FIST A DISTINCT ADVANTAGE ON THE HOME-FIELD...

-- HE'S ALREADY COMING AT ME AGAIN FROM SOMEWHERE ELSE.

FIST'S CLOSE COMBAT TECHNIQUE IS TOTALLY INSTINCTIVE--A LIFE-TIME OF SKILL AND EXPERIENCE THAT ALLOWS HIM TO LITERALLY ACT AS FAST AS HE THINKS--

--BUT THE PROPORTIONATE STRENGTH AND SPEED OF A RADIOACTIVE SPIDER IS ALL THE EQUALIZER I EVER NEED!
WHOK
YET SPIDER-MAN IS STILL JUST A FREAK PRODUCT OF ACCIDENTALLY UNLEASHED LABORATORY SCIENCE...
...WHILE IRON FIST IS THE CONTROLLED RESULT OF A NATURAL SCIENCE OF MIND AND BODY INTENTIONALLY REFINED TO AN ART FORM.
HE EVEN ROLLED WITH MY BLOW-- USING THE SOFTER FURNITURE TO ABSORB MOST OF THE IMPACT--
--BUT GIVING ME AN AN OPPORTUNITY TO TAKE THIS OUT TO THE MOONLIGHT.
PERFECT...
...NOW I CAN SAFELY RESUME THE SEARCH PROGRAMS MY VISITOR SO RUDELY INTERRUPTED EARLIER.
KLK
BUT THIS IS NOT OVER, SPIDER-MAN...

LEDGE COULD CONVENIENTLY-- BUT PAINFULLY-- *BREAK* MY FALL...

...IF MY MUSCLES WERE STILL PARALYZED.

BUT I'M BACK IN THE SWING OF THINGS *SOONER* THAN FIST COULD HAVE EXPECTED...

...THANKS TO A *LAST- SECOND* SPIDER-SENSE WARNING ABOUT HIS OH-SO-FRIENDLY SHOULDER-GRIP. BEFORE--

THWIP

GONE *ALREADY...!?*

--*KEEP* ME HERE FOR THE DURATION!

CHK

BUT MY RELUCTANT HOST SEEMED *DETERMINED* TO--

WHERE--?!

THAT CONTAINMENT CAGE WAS ONLY MEANT TO *LURE* YOU INTO *MID-LEAP* SPIDER-MAN...

215

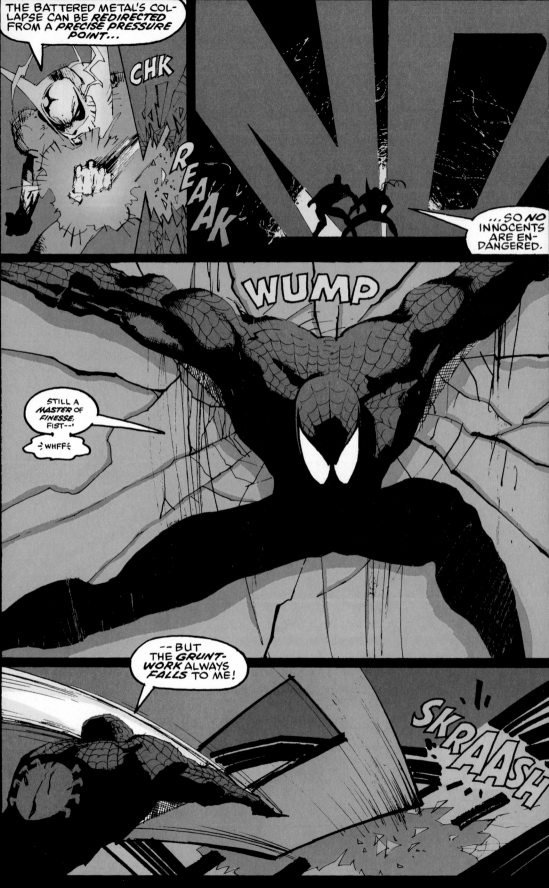

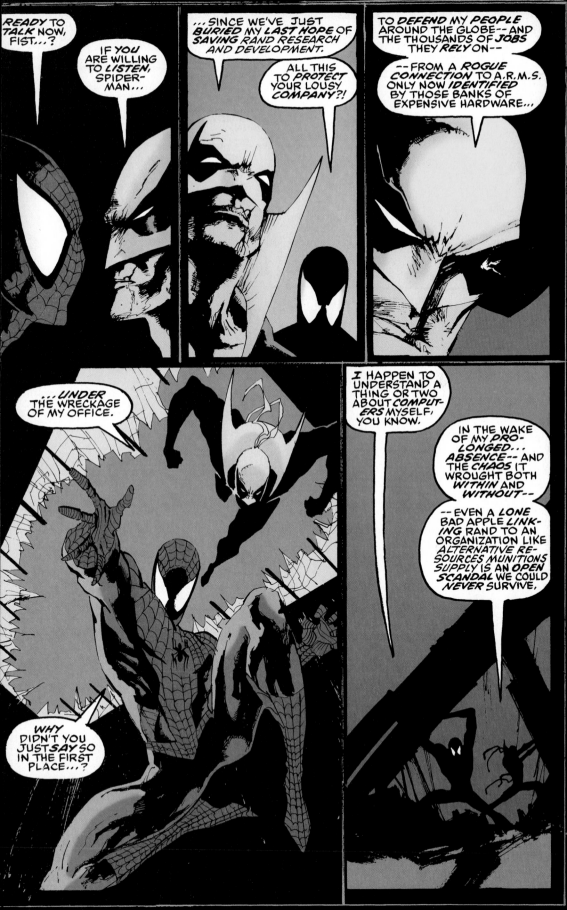

REALLY *APPRECIATE* YOUR FAITH IN ME, BUDDY...

YOU HAVE A PARTICULARLY UNIQUE *KNACK* FOR *ATTRACTING PUBLICITY,* SPIDER-MAN-- ALMOST AS IF YOU BRING IT UPON YOURSELF INTENTIONALLY--

--AND I HAVE NO RIGHT TO TAKE *RISKS* WITH OTHERS' LIVELIHOODS.

SKRTCH

DECISION'S *OUT* OF YOUR HANDS NOW, DANNY...

...WE'LL NEED *EACH OTHER* TO RECOVER ANY LOST DATA FROM THIS *SCRAP HEAP.*

I CAN DIRECT MAKESHIFT REPAIRS...

...THAT WILL REQUIRE YOUR *DELICATE TOUCH* AT THIS AWKWARD ANGLE.

IF YOU CAN *AVOID* THAT *EXPOSED POWER-CABLE* ABOVE...WHILE *SPLICING* THOSE FOUR *SILVER BACK-UP CIRCUITS* ON THE LEFT...TO THE *THIRD* MEMORY BOARD UNDERNEATH...

...IT MIGHT JUST *DE-MAGNETIZE* THE LAST ACTIVE PROGRAM LONG ENOUGH TO--

DR. DAVID CHODOSH/ STUDY ANALYST (logged in) DIVISION: CYBER-TECH LABORATORIES SUPERVISOR: DR. BYRON BOHA (logged out: indefinite sick) PROJECT STATUS: (temporarily suspended) PROJECT PURCHACES: +39%

TRACE SEQUENCE CROSS-CHECKED INCREASING AGAINST DECREASING PRODUCTION TO FIND THE *SOURCE* OF THE *SUSPICIOUS PURCHASES* SPOTLIGHTED BY *THE BUGLE...*

...POINTING RIGHT TO THE *SNAKE* IN OUR MIDST.

NOT EXACTLY *PROOF* OF INDUSTRIAL ESPIONAGE, FIST...

...BUT DR. DAVID IS CERTAINLY *BURNING* HIS CANDLE AT *BOTH* ENDS.

DESPITE A DISTINCT *LACK* OF OFFICIAL ASSIGNMENT...

TEK

...MY QUARRY'S OPERATING OUT OF ONE OF THE *SUB-BASEMENT LABS* IN THIS VERY COMPLEX.

"OUR" QUARRY, FIST...

...I'M *IN* THIS TO THE BITTER EN--

NO...

...CLEAR THE *ELEVATOR!*

SLAM

SNP

ADMIRABLE *INSTINCTS,* SPIDER-MAN...

...OUR PREY HAS LIKELY SABOTAGED *ALL* THE *NORMAL* ROUTES TO HIS NEST...

...JUST AS HE'S CAUSED THE ELEVATOR CABLE TO *SNAP*...!

STOOM

BUT THIS *ENTIRE* STRUCTURE WAS BUILT...

KRICH

219

Stan Lee presents

SPIDER-MAN

WHEN THE DAILY BUGLE'S STORY-FILE ABOUT A FLEDGLING *ILLEGAL WEAPONS CARTEL* KNOWN AS *A.R.M.S.* WAS STOLEN RIGHT FROM UNDER THE NOSE OF *PETER PARKER*...

...HIS ALTER EGO, *SPIDER-MAN*, WAS FORCED TO BATTLE A FRIEND TO PROTECT HIS JOB.

WHEN THE HOT DATA DISCS LED *DANIEL RAND* TO THE DISCOVERY OF A *TRAITOR* TO RAND RESEARCH AND DEVELOPMENT *IN LEAGUE WITH ALTERNATIVE RESOURCE MUNITION SUPPLY*...

...HIS ALTER EGO, *IRON FIST*, WAS FORCED TO BATTLE A FRIEND TO PROTECT THE JOBS OF TENS OF THOUSANDS OF INNOCENT EMPLOYEES.

BUT WHEN THE DANGEROUS TRAIL OF *DOCTOR DAVID CHODOSH* LED THEM BOTH TO THE *SUB-BASEMENT LABS* OF RAND'S MANHATTAN CORPORATE HEADQUARTERS...

...THE TWO HEROES FINALLY FOUND THE *TRUE* VILLAIN.

AMBUSH, BOYS...

TERRY KAVANAGH, WRITER JAE LEE, ARTIST TINSLEY/MORAN, COLORISTS
JOE ROSEN LETTERER DANNY FINGEROTH EDITOR TOM DeFALCO EDITOR IN CHIEF

YOU TWO HAVE-- *HAD*--A REPUTATION FOR SPEED...

...BUT I'VE GOT A *WEAPON* FOR EVERY OCCASION.

AND *SONIC-PULSES* EXPAND TO FILL A *SELF-CONTAINED* SPACE.

PLATOON TO *A.R.M.S.* CENTRAL...

SPIDER-MAN AND IRON FIST STUMBLED ONTO OUR LITTLE OPERATION, BOSS-MAN, BUT THE *WAR-SUIT* CAME THROUGH--

--AND THE ENEMY HAS BEEN *NEUTRAL-IZED.*

WRONG MOVE, CHODOSH...

...YOU WERE *ORDERED* TO RISK CAPTURE, IF NECESSARY, UNTIL WE WERE READY TO *MAXIMIZE* THE MEDIA POTENTIAL OF *ACTIVE* ENGAGEMENT.

RETURN TO BASE IMMEDIATELY...

THINK *AGAIN,* BIG SHOTS--

FSSH

SKROOM

--I QUIT!

226

229

"...WHEN PLATOON IS *FINISHED.*"

PHSS

SZZZZ

SZZZ

SZZZ

FIVE'S A *CROWD,* BOYS--!

FIST'S CLOSEST--

SPIDER-MAN DOESN'T REALIZE WHAT KIND OF *DAMAGE* A TRADITIONAL *BUZZSAW-BLADE* CAN DO...

SZZZZZ

PHSS

--BUT EVEN *HE* CAN'T AVOID A STATE-OF-THE-ART *HEAT-SEEKER* FOR LONG!

"...IN THE *WRONG* HANDS."

ZZZNKT

PHSS

IMPRESSIVE *ARMORY,* PLATOON...

237

244

"THE *BROOKLYN BRIDGE*...

"...SECOND-OLDEST BRIDGE IN ALL OF *NEW YORK*-- AND THE VERY FIRST SUSPENSION BRIDGE TO SPAN THE *EAST RIVER*, LINKING COMMERCIAL *MANHATTAN* AND RESIDENTIAL *BROOKLYN*.

"SINCE IT WAS BUILT--USING THE MOST ADVANCED ENGINEERING TECHNIQUES OF ITS DAY, AT THE PRICE OF MORE LOST LIVES THAN USUAL--

"--THIS THIN LINE OF CONCRETE AND STEEL HAS CONVEYED UNTOLD LEGIONS OF *NEW YORKERS* FROM THEIR HOMES TO THEIR JOBS AND SAFELY BACK AGAIN...

"...A *LOCAL LANDMARK* FOR WELL OVER A CENTURY.

"BUT AS OF THIS MOMENT..."

...THE *BROOKLYN BRIDGE* IS NOTHING MORE THAN A *DEATH-TRAP!*

ON THE GROUND AUTHORITIES STRUGGLED DESPERATELY TO CONTAIN THE DAMAGE DONE BY THE LONE ARMORED MAN CALLED *PLATOON*--

--BELIEVING HIM TO BE A *ROGUE* TERRORIST IN A *SINGULARLY*-DANGEROUS BATTLE-SUIT...

...UNTIL MERE SECONDS AGO*.

*LAST ISSUE.--DANNY

--AFTER THESE MESSAGES...

A PRIVATE VILLA IN MIAMI...

A BURIED OFFICE IN THE PENTAGON...

A HIDDEN JUSTICE DEPARTMENT SAFE-HOUSE...

A DIRTY CORRIDOR ON RIKER'S ISLAND...

251

A LAVISH BOARDROOM IN THE HEART OF THE CITY...

...THAT NOW SERVES AS AN IMPROMPTU CLEARING HOUSE FOR THE FLEDGLING WEAPONS MANUFACTURERS KNOWN TO THEIR EXTREMELY SELECT CLIENTELE AS *A.R.M.S.*--

--ALTERNATIVE RESOURCES MUNITIONS SUPPLY.

WE NEED MORE PHONE LINES.

WHO KNOWS *HOW* MANY POTENTIAL CUSTOMERS AREN'T GETTING THROUGH ALREADY.

MAYBE *CHODOSH* ACTUALLY DID US A *FAVOR* WHEN HE WENT *RENEGADE* WITH HIS OWN TEST-MODEL...

THE TRAITOR'S PERSONAL AMBITION--AND EMBARRASSINGLY *PUBLIC DEFEAT* AT THE HANDS OF THOSE COSTUMED MEDDLERS-- FORCED AN EARLY UNVEILING OF *ALL* THE PLATOONS...

...SO WE HAVE NO CHOICE BUT TO TRY AND *TURN* THE RESULTING MEDIA ATTENTION TO OUR ADVANTAGE.

BUT IF THE REST OF OUR PROTOTYPES CAN *TAKE* THAT BELOVED BRIDGE-- OVER THE *VERY* DEAD BODIES OF SPIDER-MAN AND IRON FIST--

--THE PLATOON *WAR-SUIT* WILL TRULY SELL *ITSELF!*

252

THEN TAKE IT TO THE *RIVER!*

BUT THEY ARE *NOT* FOLLOWING US--

UKK

ZZZ ZZZ ZZZ

SPLSSH

"...IS MORE THAN ENOUGH TO *KILL* ANYONE."

PROBABLY FIGURE A *TWO-HUNDRED-AND-SEVENTY FOOT DROP...*

SPIDER-MAN AND IRON FIST ARE *DOWN.*

SO WITH POLICE *S.W.A.T.* TEAMS STILL IN *DISARRAY* ON THE NIGHT-DESERTED MANHATTAN SIDE OF THE BRIDGE SINCE THE INITIAL STRIKE...

...NO ONE STANDS BETWEEN THE ARMY OF PLATOONS AND THEIR APPARENT DESTINATION-- THE *POPULATED STREETS* OF BUSTLING BROOKLYN!

NEWS 7

AND AS LONG AS THE PLATOONS CONTINUE TO TOLERATE OUR PRESENCE--

--THIS STATION WILL BRING YOU *UP-TO-THE-MINUTE COVERAGE* OF THE CRISIS WE'RE CALLING "*MARCH ON BROOKLYN*"...!

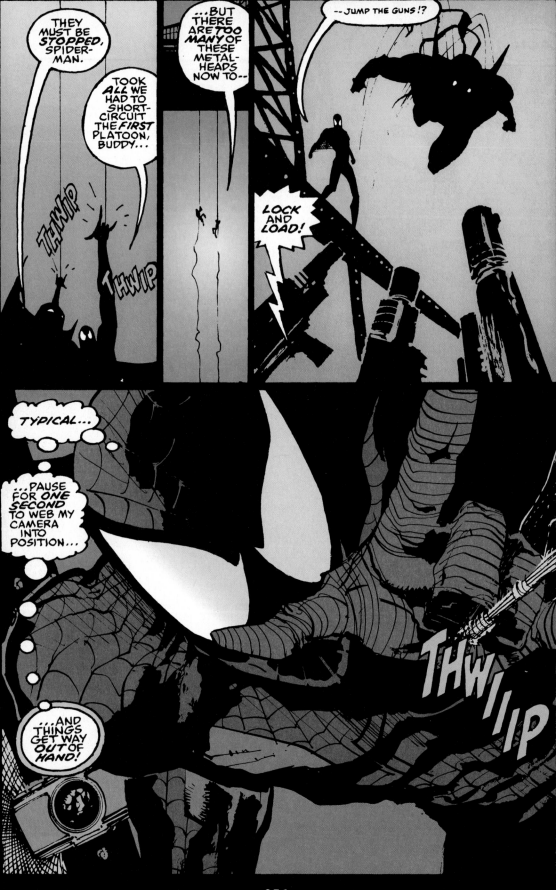

260

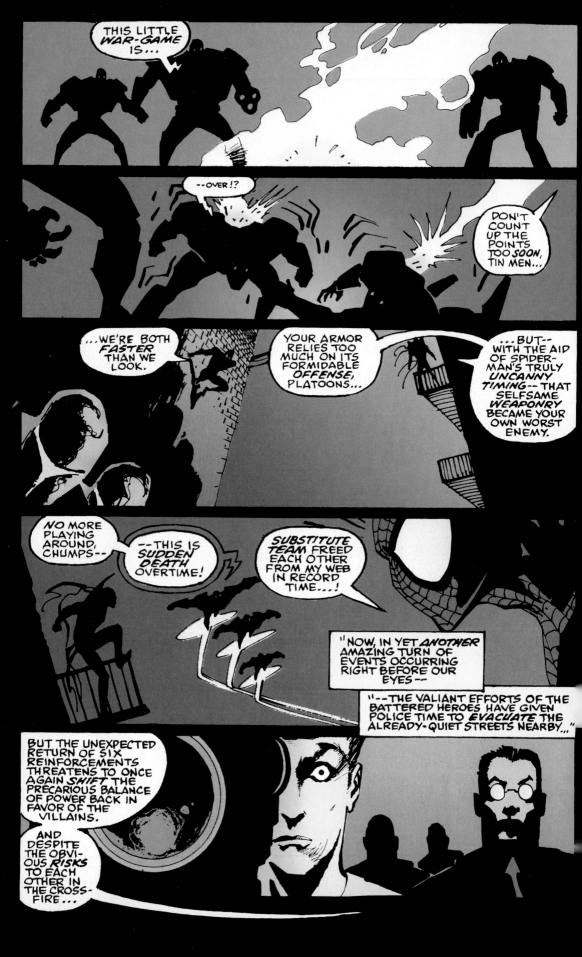

"...THESE PLATOONS HAVE CLEARLY *TARGETED* THE VERY CHAMPIONS WHO BRAVELY REPELLED THEIR RUTHLESS 'MARCH ON BROOKLYN.'"

DO IT, FIST--!

"YOU MAKE FINE *BAIT*, SPIDER-MAN..."

WHAT--?!

BOOM

KRNG

...BUT A BIG GUN LIKE THIS CAN BE PUT TO FAR *BETTER* USE--

"--*CLEANING* OUT THE NEIGHBORHOOD."

"WE'RE WITNESSING THE TRUE DEFINITION OF *HEROISM* IN ACTION HERE TODAY, FOLKS!"

SKRAOOM

"IN AN ALMOST-INHUMAN DISPLAY OF TRUST, SPIDER-MAN CONFIDENTLY *LURED* ONE OF THE BLOODTHIRSTY ASSASSINS INTO FIRING A POWERFUL *PLASMA-BOLT*..."

"...THAT IRON FIST HAS PRECISELY *REDIRECTED*-- WITH UNERRING ACCURACY--TOWARDS THE *VULNERABLE CORNERSTONE* OF AN *UNOCCUPIED BUILDING-IN-PROGRESS!*"

SKROO--

LOOK OUT!

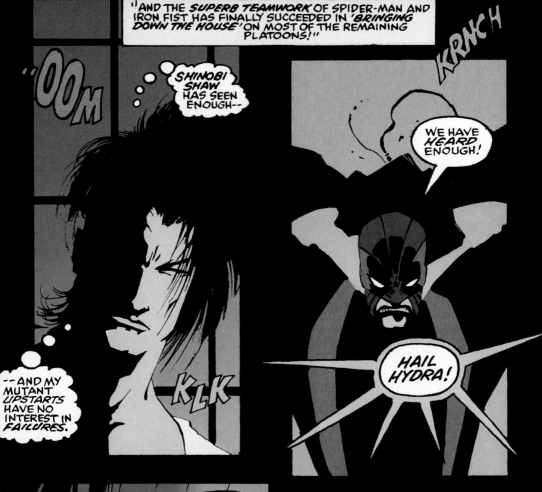

'OOM

SHINOBI SHAW HAS SEEN ENOUGH--

KLK

--AND MY MUTANT *UPSTARTS* HAVE NO INTEREST IN *FAILURES.*

KRNCH

WE HAVE *HEARD* ENOUGH!

HAIL HYDRA!

ENOUGH!

BRIIP

MASTREX SAT-YR-9 HAS NO TIME FOR SUCH NONSENSE!

...ON MOST OF THE REMAINING PLATOONS!

TELEVISION DISTRACT-ING YOU, *FISK--*

TEK

-- OR YOU FINALLY FINISHED RUNNING UP THE GOVERN-MENT *PROTECTION PROGRAM'S* PHONE BILL?

BACK TO YOUR CELL, "GAUNTLET"--

--NO MORE TELEPHONE PRIVILEGES UNTIL THE END OF THE MONTH.

TAX-PAYERS WILL NEVER EVEN REALIZE...

...HOW MUCH MONEY THEY JUST SAVED.

THE SLUG HAS AN EXPANDING CRIMINAL EMPIRE TO RUN--

--AND THIS IS A COMPLETE

ANYONE KNOW THE GOING RATE FOR SCRAP METAL THESE DAYS?

-- SO THE REST OF THESE SPLATOONS *OVERLOAD* EACH OTHER ON CONTACT.

AND A *SYNCHRONIZED FEEDBACK LOOP* BETWEEN THEIR DUPLICATE ARMORS WILL *KEEP* THEM THAT WAY UNTIL THEY *RUST.*

CONGRATU-LATIONS, HEROES...

ZTTZ

TZZT

ZTTZ

...NOW THE READERS OF THE *DAILY BUGLE* HAVE SOME QUES-TIONS FOR IRON FIST ABOUT HOW THIS ALL *BEGAN.*

WHAT IS *IMPORTANT* --MS. *CUSHING,* I BELIEVE...?--

GOOD PRESS NEVER LASTS FOR LONG...

...BUT *DANNY'S* COMMITTED TO *PROTECTING RAND RESEARCH*-- AND THE THOUSANDS OF INNOCENT FAMILIES WORLD-WIDE THAT DEPEND ON IT FOR THEIR LIVELIHOODS--

"WHEN THIS FIRST STARTED, I JUST WANTED TO SAVE *ONE* JOB--*MINE*--FROM MY VOLA-TILE CITY EDI-TOR'S WRATH...

"...AND MY *AUTOMATIC CAMERA* MIGHT ACTU-ALLY DO THE TRICK FOR EVERYONE.

--IS THAT IT IS FINALLY *FINISHED* ONCE AND FOR ALL.

--FROM THE *CONSEQUENCES* OF THE LONE DR. *DAVID CHODOSH'S* UNAUTHORIZED INVOLVEMENT IN THE DEVELOPMENT OF THE PLATOON BATTLE-ARMOR.

"IF, AND *ONLY* IF, *KATE* IS WILLING TO *FORGET* ABOUT THE INCRIMINA-TING EVIDENCE I ORIGINALLY *BORROWED* FROM HER-- AND FIST *STOLE* FROM ME--

"-- IN EXCHANGE FOR PETER *PARKER'S PHOTO SCOOP* FROM THE *HEART* OF THE FAILED 'MARCH ON BROOKLYN'.

OF COURSE, *WHOEVER* ORGANIZED THIS BIZARRE *ASSAULT...*

MARVEL FANFARE #33 PINUP BY IAN AKIN & BRIAN GARVEY

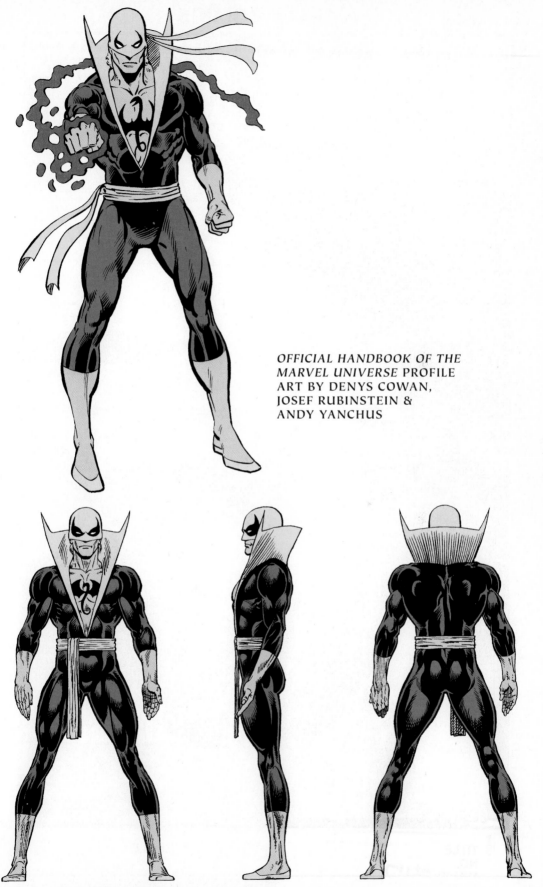

OFFICIAL HANDBOOK OF THE MARVEL UNIVERSE PROFILE
ART BY DENYS COWAN,
JOSEF RUBINSTEIN &
ANDY YANCHUS

OFFICIAL HANDBOOK OF THE MARVEL UNIVERSE: MASTER EDITION
PROFILE ART BY KEITH POLLARD, JOSEF RUBINSTEIN & ANDY YANCHUS

MARVEL® COMICS

BACK-COVER ART BY STEVE LIGHTLE